BRILLIANT B

BRILLIANT BUSINESS IDEAS

The Entrepreneur's Guide
to Profitable Creativity

JOSEPH BENN

bookshaker

First Published in Great Britain 2011
by www.BookShaker.com

© Copyright Joseph Benn

All rights reserved. No part of this publication may be reproduced, stored in or introduced into a retrieval system, or transmitted, in any form, or by any means (electronic, mechanical, photocopying recording or otherwise) without the prior written permission of the publisher.

This book is sold subject to the condition that it shall not, by way of trade or otherwise, be lent, resold, hired out, or otherwise circulated without the publisher's prior consent in any form of binding or cover other than that in which it is published and without a similar condition including this condition being imposed on the subsequent purchaser.

*This book is dedicated to my Grandparents:
John Edward and Agnes Mary
Ernie and Helen Benn*

PRAISE

"We live in the Age of The Ideas. And it is the Unreasonable Power of Creativity that makes the difference. This book will help you and your team get there"
Kevin Roberts
CEO, Saatchi & Saatchi

"The best business ideas are those that enable you to build on past experience to bring about positive, sustainable, profitable change to the lives of others. The simplest are always the best. This book will help you to better than best – brilliant in fact!"
Robert Ashton
Author of How to Start Your Business – for Entrepreneurs

"If you have the ambition but not the idea then this book is the answer! It will give you simple yet powerful techniques enabling you to come up with viable business ideas centred around you as an individual. Used properly this book will turn your brain into a business ideas factory!"
Simon Hazeldine
Bestselling author of Bare Knuckle Negotiating and Bare Knuckle Selling

"Some really interesting methods taught all the way through – I know if I had applied some of the principles you talk of to my business life then I may have saved money on some of my mistakes! You talk through the set-up of a business (or generation of an idea) in a 'logical' manner that encourages people to leave no stone unturned. It's quite easy to run away with an idea and when you look back you think 'actually I wish I had looked into this just a little bit more before setting out…'

I could see it being useful to people wanting to start in business but with no idea yet, people setting up in business who want to test a few ideas or also to a business coach working with people setting out in business.

A real eye-opener with regards to protecting ideas and copy write laws on both the UK and world front.

15 is my favourite chapter. Being creative yourself is one thing, ensuring you get the most out the workforce is another. I'd say this is a really good model for growing companies to follow when developing policies, throughout creative training days and in other communication with the workforce and customers too."

Peter Harrison
Co-Owner of FGH Security and Dragons' Den Winner

ACKNOWLEDGEMENTS

THANK YOU TO MY FAMILY who have put up with my eccentricity for 33 years without too much complaint. I love you all very much.

Thanks to Rintu Basu, who kept me on the straight and narrow and helped me to achieve a lifelong ambition. If you could remove the nightmares now, that would be great, Rintu!

Thank you to Simon Hazeldine for his words of encouragement.

Thank you to Joe Gregory for agreeing to publish this book and to Lucy McCarraher for bearing with me whilst I worked out how to use a computer properly.

CONTENTS

Praise
Acknowledgements
Contents
Foreword
Introduction

One: Creativity	13
Why creativity is vital	13
Creativity – what is it?	16
Why you need a box!	17
Optimum Conditions for Creativity	20
Two: Ideas Generation Process	23
Ideas Generation	23
Ideas Checker	27
Ideas Implementation	28
Three: Sources of Ideas	31
Passions	32
Hobbies	33
Anger/Frustration	34
Necessity	34
Four: The Ideas Matrix	37
Exercise	42
Case Study	43
More case studies	51

Five: Awkward Questions	55
How Questions	58
Why Questions	59
Where Questions	60
What Questions	61
Miscellaneous Questions	64
Case Study	65
Exercise	67
Second Exercise	68
Six: The Ideas Heist	71
Exercise	74
Second Exercise	75
Seven: Negative Thinking	77
Case Study: Robin	84
Exercise	87
Eight: Ideas Mapping	89
Case Study	92
Another Case Study	98
The importance of Questions	104
One Final Tip	105
Exercise	106
Nine: Some General Rules for Ideas Generation	107
Ten: Ideas Checker	111
Personal	114
Ethics, Values and Morals	114
Time	115
Are you the right person?	115
Partners	117
Market	117

Where is your market going?	118
Competitors	118
Financial	119
Protection	121
Marketing	122
Supply Chain	124
Other Resources	126
Eleven: Implementation	129
Business Plan	129
Allies and Mentors	134
Action	136
Networking	136
Marketing	138
Twelve: How To Protect Your Idea	139
Design Rights	139
Copyright	140
Trademarks	140
Patents	142
Trade Secrets	143
Case Study: Robin and Total Strategy	144
Case Study: Rick	149
Thirteen: How To Sell Your Idea	155
Protection	155
Proof that the idea works	156
Case Study	160
Fourteen: How To Encourage Employees	165
A System	172
The Creative Manager	175

Fifteen: Personal Creativity for Business	179
Idea Mapping with Employees	179
Case Study	181
Ideas Mapping with yourself	183
The Five-Sided Technique	184
Perceptual Positioning	186
Case Study	188
The Perfect X	191
Male into Female and vice versa	191
Sixteen: Final Words	193

Resources
About The Author

FOREWORD

I HAVE KNOWN JOE FOR a number of years. I really got to know him when he attended one of my NLP practitioner courses and what has impressed me most about him is his unique way of applying the material he learned. This great book is just one small example of the genius of this man.

If you had asked me before reading this book, does the world really need another book on creativity I would have categorically said no. Here is how I changed my mind.

I have a frustration about many of the books I have read about creativity. They go on about how important creativity is in business, they give great examples of the successful use of creativity but in the end the best exercises they have amount to talking a walk in a park or an art gallery, making free associations or wearing silly hats in meetings. Whilst I think these are useful exercises I can't help feeling that there is more to creativity.

I remember a few years ago coaching an MD of a large organisation who was full of frustration. The main issue was, in his words, "We don't need wild and wacky creativity; we need ideas that will help us save money or make money. But I just can't get my team to think inside the box for a change." This MD said it the most eloquently but this is a common frustration I have seen in leadership teams where everyone is off doing great creative things and no one is looking after the core business.

If I were to pick two things that I drum into NLP Practitioners, they would be:

- If you want to replicate success work you need to deconstruct the process
- The quality of your results are based on the quality of the questions you ask

Joe has done a great thing by taking these concepts and applying them to creativity. Skilfully Joe has deconstructed and demonstrated the process of how to be creative in business. He has then developed sequences of questions that simultaneously allow you to keep your eye on the ball whilst still unleashing your creativity.

I think ideas are worth nothing because hundreds of people have hundreds of ideas. Not even good ideas are worth anything until they are implemented. So how would it be if you had a book that could show you how to generate ideas, useful ideas, ideas you could even build a business on? And then the book goes further by showing you how to develop, protect and implement those ideas. A book like that could, for some people, be the start of the multi million pound empire, a way to accelerate their career or simply a way of being more successful, productive and happy at work.

Does the world really need another book on business creativity? The answer is a resounding YES, but only if it can show you how to create, develop, protect and implement ideas to further your goals, career or business. Luckily that is the book you are holding in your hands.

Rintu Basu
Bestselling author of the
'*Persuasion Skills Black Book*'
www.thenlpcompany.com

INTRODUCTION

ENTERPRISE IS VERY FASHIONABLE AT the moment. Entrepreneurs have become celebrities and shows such as *Dragon's Den* and *The Apprentice*, (the second one is more concerned with corporate snakes but we'll accept it for now), signal the public's fascination with enterprise and a certain perception of the business world. With the current economic situation many people will be facing unemployment and redundancy. Now is a great time to start your own business! Providing, that is, you have the right idea, the right skills and a bit of luck. There are hundreds, if not thousands, of business books out there most of them concerned with developing a business and making it a success. This book is about the step before that – actually coming up with a business idea that is not only viable but motivates and excites you. The majority of people come up with ideas but don't follow them through, which can be blamed on a number of things, two of which are – a lack of emotional involvement with the idea and a lack of knowledge. When you apply the techniques you will learn in this book, you will come up with ideas that matter to you and be shown ways of checking their viability. Its then up to you to supply the motivation and determination but getting motivated is a lot easier if you find the idea exciting.

This book is for people who want to set-up their own business, full-time or part-time, but lack an actual idea. For a large number of people this is the number-one stumbling block to getting started. The saying: "there's nothing new under the sun," is true to some extent but there are still plenty of ways to make money and new markets are developing all the time. The internet, for example, has given everyone in the western world the ability to have their own online business and dip their toe in the entrepreneurial pool. This book will give you some very easy to use techniques that are proven to work, supercharging your creativity and *turning your mind into a business ideas factory*. These techniques require nothing more than a piece of paper and something to write with. Once you have practiced them a few times you probably won't even need paper and writing implements as you will be able to do most of them in your head. *No matter whether or not you consider yourself to be creative these techniques, used correctly as detailed in this book, will work for you – they cannot fail!* There are pluses and minuses to setting up your own business and you need to be aware of them before you start.

Advantages

- All the rewards come to you – you get all the fruits of your labour (minus costs and what the taxman takes, of course).

INTRODUCTION

- It's very exciting and fulfilling running your own business and a massive learning experience. Being able to implement your own vision the way you want to and realising your ambition (small or large) will be a fantastic feeling.

- People will respect and admire you for having taken the risk – as noted at the beginning of this book there is a growing awareness of and respect for entrepreneurs in our society.

- It may seem contradictory but in some ways you are actually more secure as a business owner than you are working for someone else. You have full control and your destiny is in your hands. No faceless corporate high-flier or consultant can make you redundant or add stress to your job.

- Running your own business will equip you with experience and skills that, in the event of you deciding to close the business or it failing, will be valuable to a potential employer.

- If you've ever had the misfortune to work for an incompetent or uninspiring boss, then you will appreciate the freedom that setting up your own business gives you.

Disadvantages

- You, your family and partner take all the risks – will your family put up with your absence as you sacrifice time with them in favour of the business? Will your family understand if finances become tight and they can't go on the annual holiday?

- It can be very lonely and isolating – unless a lot of your friends are self employed or have their own businesses it is unlikely that they will understand the path that you have taken. It is likely that your level of contact with your social circle will go down as you work all hours (similar to the loss of time with your family). Not all of your social circle will find this easy to accept and you may well lose friends.

- You will have more than a few sleepless nights. At the end of the day everything comes down to you, so if you don't think you can put up with the stress and the worry of running your own business then you need to consider whether you're the right person for it.

- If your business fails people will tell you "I told you so." People like to see others fail. Can you put up with the sniggers and them telling you "I told you so," if your business does not work out the way you want?

INTRODUCTION

- You have to be a jack of all trades – most of the time you will have to do everything yourself. You will be your own marketing department, your own finance department, your own buyer and your own planner. You need to honestly appraise your skills and experience. Work out what you can learn, what you already know and what you definitely need to outsource.

- You will not have a regular guaranteed income – if you're used to a monthly salary then a sudden drop in income will be a huge shock. There may be times when you make a lot and other times when you make very little. You may need to make adjustments to your lifestyle to cater for this.

- No benefits package – benefits that you may have previously enjoyed by right as an employee, even something as simple as holiday entitlement, go out of the window and you always have to consider the effect on the business before deciding to go away for a few days or contribute to a pension scheme.

If those disadvantages have not put you off then here are the views of some entrepreneurs who have set-up their own businesses. None of them are millionaires by any means and they work much harder than the average working Joe:

Miguel

"To say it's been hard is an understatement! At the beginning I had a partner and the two of us would have to get up at five in the morning to ensure that our product was ready on time. The hours were very long – it was often close to midnight before I got into bed – and I had new skills to learn, such as finance, marketing, negotiation and sales. Every day was scary and it was a learning experience. I made so many mistakes in the early days, which was extremely costly! There was a large amount of worry and stress but there was also a lot of excitement. I've been running my own business for over two years now and while there are still times when I get scared and there's still things I worry about, I am very proud and very happy. I have my own business! I don't think that I could work for anyone else now. The level of responsibility and control that I have I don't think I could gain elsewhere. Basically it's up to me whether I succeed or fail. "

Faye

"It's definitely the hardest thing I've ever done. There's so much to think about that at the end of the day I'm knackered. If I couple that with the fact that my business is not quite ready to support me full-time, which means that I also have a part-time job, I suddenly realise that I'm spending most of my time working. I am enjoying it but I won't lie; there are days

INTRODUCTION

where I yearn for the simple nine to five. I'm going to carry on, though, as things are getting better and I can see a light at the end of the tunnel where I can give up my part-time job and work full-time on something that's meaningful to me."

This book is also for people who already have an idea but don't know what to do with it.

We've seen *Dragon's Den* on the television, where someone goes before the Dragons with an idea that for a second sounds fantastic before reality hits home and you suddenly realise that it's actually insane. It's all the more painful when the person announces that they have spent their children's inheritance and dedicated ten years of their life to developing their idea/business/product and its obvious after a quick analytical look that the idea is doomed to failure.

This book will give you a series of tools that will allow you to check whether or not your idea is actually viable, and whether or not it's the right idea for you.

Most of these tools won't take long to apply and use. For example, Ellie had a number of ideas but wasn't sure what to do with them and she found the Ideas Checker invaluable.

Ellie

"When you've got an idea you really want someone to tell you whether it will work or not. I shared my ideas with friends and family and they were all very encouraging but what I really needed to do was to talk to someone in the know. The Ideas Checker allowed me to do my own research and the more research I did the more excited I became because the idea became more solid. It was actually empowering to learn what I had to look at, do my own research and form my own opinions."

This book is also for those people who already have their own businesses and need a new product or service but are lacking ideas. People in this situation are often so involved with the day-today running of the business that they can't see the wood for the trees. You'll also be aware that some companies and entrepreneurs, such as Dyson as a notable example, are constantly coming up with new ideas and products. *This book will give you some techniques and principles that you can apply to an existing product or use to come up with a totally new product.*

The book will also show you how to help your employees be more creative and how to provide an environment in which creative individuals can thrive and feel appreciated. Businesses with creative workforces experience the following benefits:

- They create more products and services
- They keep on improving their existing products and services
- They make more money
- They gain more respect in their industry

INTRODUCTION

In the current economic situation all of the above will be welcomed by most businesses. When things start to get hard, many businesses restrict their activities, cutting all marketing and training – in-house creative thinking can be done extremely quickly and the results can be out of all proportion to the resources dedicated to it. Do not neglect creative thinking in your business.

The book is also for career-minded people who want to get noticed as ideas people and want to add value to their company.

The processes you'll learn in this book will give you an edge over your colleagues, enabling you to come up with a whole host of ideas for, say, marketing campaigns or new products.

What are the benefits to being more creative in your career? Well there are two big ones – firstly that you will do a better job and secondly that you will get noticed by your bosses. Creative thinkers have more ideas than their colleagues – good and bad – and they tend to have them quicker. It has also been proven that the more creative you are, the happier and more fulfilled you will be in your job.

Some of the creative techniques demonstrated in this book occur quite naturally in some people. For example, James worked in the defence industry as a buyer for nearly five years. A highly creative thinker, his unique solutions to the problems and challenges faced by his team, brought him to the attention of his manager.

James

"One of the most exciting things I realised is that creativity has no boundaries. I didn't necessarily need to know too much about the subject or thing in question to apply creativity to it. The best example of this is when I was in a design meeting for a new piece of equipment. I'm a buyer not a designer and not particularly technically minded but I was at the meeting because I would be buying the materials for this piece of equipment. I listened to the designers discussing the issues they had which was essentially that the equipment needed to be made smaller. I was practically dropping off to sleep when for some reason I asked myself a question and sat bolt upright in my seat. Without thinking, I voiced the question. There was a silence in the room as all the designers looked at each other and pondered my question. It went on for so long that I got embarrassed and started to apologise for asking a stupid question when one of the designers grudgingly admitted that he hadn't thought of that before. The manager who was running the meeting asked him why not and the guy said it was because it had always been done that way. The next day I was walking down the corridor when that same manager stopped and introduced me to the managing director of the company as the guy who had come up with a solution to a major problem. Since then, by using the same techniques, I've managed to conquer loads of challenges and have got a name for myself as an ideas guy and problem solver."

Connected to this is a chapter on being an effective creative manager/boss looking at how you can use creative thinking to be a better problem solver, communicate better with your staff and encourage them to up their creativity levels.

The book is also for people who want to improve their creativity levels and learn how to apply it to various areas of their lives.

It is about creativity in business with a particular focus on coming up with business ideas and new products, for which I have selected particular creative thinking techniques and developed a particular structure.

These techniques have been applied to a wide variety of contexts – not just business – but it is up to you to decide how to do this and you can use them in any way you want.

For example, one student who learned these techniques from my website used them to plan his essays:

"I initially used these techniques because I wanted to come up with a business idea but I rapidly realised that I could also use them to write my essays. I'm studying Politics and English Literature. In English Literature you often have to look at themes and symbolism within novels and poems, analyse them and form an argument. Using a slightly modified version of the ideas matrix technique I managed to make a whole load of connections between novels and poetry on the reading list that my department set. On one occasion I had an essay question that I didn't understand totally; I mean I really had to concentrate on it. Using the five-sided problem I managed to re-word the question making it a hell of a lot easier to answer. I then used the idea-mapping technique to actually plan and write the essay. I actually enjoyed doing it – being able to see all these different links and coming up with interesting and at times original viewpoints really made me feel better about my degree and earned me praise and high marks from my tutor."

You are limited only by your imagination – it is up to you how you use these creative techniques. In this book is everything you need to come up with an idea and ensure that it is viable. It is recommended that you follow the guidelines and carry out each exercise as you come to it, to ensure that the techniques and processes are embedded in your mind.

We're going to kick things off with a look at creativity.

ONE
CREATIVITY

IN THIS CHAPTER YOU WILL learn the following:

- Why creativity is vital in life and business
- What creativity actually is, why it's the same as telling a joke and why anyone can do it.
- Why thinking outside the box is bad when it comes to generating business ideas and what happens when there is no structure behind creative thinking.
- Optimum conditions for creativity.

Knowing the above will place you ahead of most people and automatically heighten your creativity levels as Fran found: When I realised what creativity actually was I suddenly realised that I was really creative and started to notice when I was being creative – it's a circle. I think that a lot of people don't believe that they're creative I certainly didn't. Knowing that I was a creative person really helped with my confidence.

Why creativity is vital

It is fair to say that without creativity mankind may well not be here today. It is only by using his capacity for creativity that mankind managed to overcome the countless problems that have faced him since the cave age. That mankind has always had an appreciation of creativity and has individuals who display it in spades, can be seen from the ancient cave paintings. From staying warm in winter to getting food and outwitting his enemies, cavemen had to be hugely creative. In more recent times putting a man on the moon and sending men down into the deepest parts of the ocean are all examples of man's creative spirit in action. Creativity has been vital to mankind's survival and will no doubt continue to be so. The value put by society in creative individuals can be seen in the almost universal adoration of the genius of such artists as Leonardo Da Vinci, Michelangelo and others.

To be healthy mankind must find an outlet for his creativity and thus produces works of art, architecture and even such things as graffiti. Being creative makes us relax and much happier as people. There is a joy in being creative that is almost childlike. All of mankind's greatest achievements, for example landing a man on the moon, came about through creative thinking and extensive action.

People who have been identified as "ideas people" are valued in our society. Those people who are creative thinkers are seen as something special – if they can back this up by implementing their creativity. The creative thinker has a massive advantage over his peers. If you can do something quicker, cheaper and more effectively than your colleagues then you are more certain to succeed. Children are naturally creative

CREATIVITY

thinkers but as they get older and go through the education system they seem to lose their creativity and as they become adults they can become rigid in their thinking. It has been theorised that by the time you become an adult you have lost up to ninety-five percent of your creativity! This is not only tragic, it's criminal! I don't know if the effects of reduced creativity levels in a person can be measured but I am willing to bet that none of the effects will be positive. If nothing else, this book will help you regain that lost creativity and in taking you through the exercises will enable you to become one of those rare creatures – a truly creative thinker who can apply creativity in all areas of life.

What do we mean by creativity? We've all heard terms such as creative thinking and thinking out of the box but they have been over-used and so clichéd as to have become meaningless. The number of books that have been written about creative thinking can be divided into two types. Those that are so boring and dry they actually drain all creativity from your soul and those that seem to be written by hippies who urge you to think like a child and run through a forest naked, which is somehow supposed to inspire creativity! The truth is that there is nothing particularly hard or magical about being creative! Once you know how, it's simple!

Creativity – what is it?

Let's ask another question. Why is telling a joke and coming up with a new idea the same thing?

Because they are both about making connections that weren't there before. They both make connections and links between disparate things. You make a connection between disparate things and get a laugh (joke) or you make those links and come up with something new (idea). Comedians tend to be highly intelligent, creative people. One of my favourites is Billy Connolly. He is particularly talented at interrupting himself while telling a story to relate a second tale, which he then connects with the original story to get the laugh. Entrepreneurs are often similar – they will make connections that others do not. Class clowns are also the same – that troublesome kid who makes all the others laugh! He or she is making new connections – you might want to start looking at him or her in a different way. Coming from a family of teachers, I have heard time and again of former pupils who were the class clown and written-off (as was Richard Branson) who have gone on to start businesses and done much better for themselves than the class genius. It does seem that creativity and being a maverick often go together. Einstein was a genius at making new connections. He often said that his imagination was more useful to him and contributed more to the discoveries he made than his mathematical ability. For example the theory of relativity came from him imagining himself riding on a beam of light.

Why you need a box!

So now we're clear about creativity and what it is. On its own, however, it is not enough for those of us who want to develop business ideas. We need to ensure that those ideas we come up with will actually work in the real world and not just in our imaginations. We do this by being creative within a structure. It's ok to "think outside the box" but for an idea to be useful we need to think within a very particular box. As mentioned in the introduction there have been plenty of times on the television series *Dragon's Den* when someone has made such a bizarre, insane presentation that it's hard to believe anyone could think it was a good idea. The issues with the idea seem obvious to everyone outside the business. "What was he thinking" is a constant refrain in our home as we watch this and I imagine it's the same across the country; let's be honest – its one of the reasons we watch the show! The issue of course is that that person wasn't thinking – at least not in the right way. They came up with a wild idea and plunged straight into making it a reality without doing any research or development. Here are examples of some ideas that came into being without being developed in a specific structure or without the owner taking the time to develop them:

Sinclair C5

Designed, created and launched by the entrepreneur Sir Clive Sinclair the C5 was a radical vehicle; a pedal tricycle that was assisted by a battery. Sir Clive believed that it would revolutionise commuting – especially in places like London – that it would reduce traffic pollution and help people get fit.

The C5 however suffered from a number of problems. First of all its design. It was not designed to appeal to any one group of people and looked slightly ridiculous. Coupled with this the photo of its designer – an older man – riding around in it was a massive PR disaster that would have put most young people off. Secondly, due to its low, close to the road, design it was seen as impractical and dangerous – other road users – particularly in busy cities such as London – would have massive difficulty seeing you, which could lead to some very nasty accidents. These problems led to the C5 becoming the butt of jokes and it was a failure. This was in the 1980s. I wonder if the C5 would be better received today in a world more concerned with the environment and our effect on it. The C5 was an idea that was maybe ahead of its time and one that certainly sounds good on paper but ultimately the end result was not viable at the time.

Pets.com

You can probably remember the dot-com boom. People poured millions into some very weird business ideas that they would probably have laughed at if they hadn't been on the internet. Take Pets.com. It sold pet supplies to retail companies and its talking sock puppet was massively popular in America being used by the Super Bowl as part of an advertisement. While Pets.com's marketing was fantastic the actual business model has some fairly large holes in it. For example pet owners had to wait at least a couple of days to receive the goods they had bought. Pets.com in order to be competitive weren't able to charge the full shipping prices on some of their goods so at times they didn't make any profit. Pets.com folded rather quickly. If the owners had asked themselves some simple questions the chances are that things would have been very different.

Flooz.com was one of a whole host of online businesses that popped up during the dot-com bubble. Designed as an online currency and fronted by Whoopi Goldberg in television commercials (which apparently cost over eight million dollars) it reportedly lost over fifty million dollars of investment and unwittingly sold some of its currency to fraudsters. Why did it fail? Because no-one actually wanted to use online currency. Most people were happy with the currency they already had. Think about it! It takes a lot of trust for most people to use another currency and the internet was relatively new – people were still suspicious of it. Beenz.com a similar model went the same way.

This book will give you a specific structure which if you work within it and carry out the necessary work will help you to avoid the fate of the examples above.

Before we come to that however let's look at the optimum conditions for creativity.

Optimum Conditions for Creativity

Everyone is different but there are some common factors that you want to bear in mind when having a creative thinking session:

- **Eat and drink well** – if you are hungry then all you will be able to think about is food and your concentration and creativity levels will drop. Likewise if your diet is poor then your brain will not get the necessary vitamins and sugars it needs to work at optimum levels. Some of the techniques in this book require a high level of concentration so be sure you are giving your brain the best chance it has. Keep hydrated – when you become dehydrated your performance levels drop dramatically.

- **Sleep and rest well** – it has been scientifically proven that if you are not getting enough rest and sleep then you can't think properly and your creativity levels will drop dramatically. The amount of sleep you need is personal to you –

you will know whether or not you are well rested and thinking clearly.

- **Time** – a creative thinking session should last no more than forty-five minutes. Any longer and you will start to lose focus and motivation unless there has been a steady influx of ideas. If you're working in a group get one of them to be timekeeper and get them to be strict with it.

- **Keep fit and healthy** – a fit, healthy individual is one who thinks more calmly and with more clarity. Being fit and healthy will help in all areas of your life.

- **Group** – Working in a group is a good way of supercharging your creative thinking sessions. As long as you have the right people and they agree to follow the rules and processes in this book then you will be amazed at the amount and quality of ideas produced. There should be no more than five people in the group.

So now we know about creativity, let's learn about the ideas generation process.

BRILLIANT BUSINESS IDEAS

TWO

IDEAS GENERATION PROCESS

BY KNOWING EACH PART OF the ideas generation process you will find that your creative thinking sessions will be much more productive and focused. By using this structure you avoid overlap and the loss of momentum caused by getting caught up in issues and details that would be better dealt with at a different time. If you are to get the best results from this book then it is vital you follow this process.

The Ideas Generation Process has three parts to it:

- Ideas Generation
- Ideas Checker
- Ideas Implementation

Ideas Generation

For many people this is the most exciting part. You use the techniques outlined in this book to generate ideas. You may come up with one idea or many but it's important to let them flow and not judge them. At this stage we need to leave our critical faculties out. A good example of this is an ideas generation workshop, which was held with some seventeen–year-old students. They were taught the Ideas Matrix (which you shall be introduced to later) and then asked to relate some of the business ideas that they had generated. Two students came up with the idea of offering commuters a lap-dancing service on the railway platform when their train was late. There was uproar when they related the idea – mainly from the seventeen-year-old girls who were somewhat mollified when the boys told them there would be male lap-dancers for the women passengers. I was running the workshop myself and totally pooh-poohed the idea so, feeling slightly uncomfortable under the beady glare of the students' teacher who seemed to be holding me personally responsible for the students' lap-dancing idea, I moved on. A couple of weeks later I was reading a newspaper and saw something that made me chuckle. A company in Europe had been set-up offering dancing lessons on the platform to people whose trains were late. Not exactly the same idea but it did make me feel that I had been too quick in judging the students so harshly. So the most important rule for this part of the process is: do not judge the ideas that are created. The second rule is to make sure you record the ideas either by noting them down or even, if it is at all possible, to film the entire session if you are doing it in a group – it is amazing what can be missed when people are discussing things. If everyone is comfortable with this then film the session and play it back towards the end to see if there are any pearls of creativity you might have missed. The best sessions are those where people get animated and all talk at once. Aim to get as much value from your sessions as possible. If it is not possible to film or record the sessions then make sure someone is taking notes and gets everyone's suggestions down. Another thing to consider when doing this session is ideas protection. Without wanting to make you paranoid don't ever do an ideas generation session with someone you don't trust. This is perhaps the biggest down-side to generating ideas in a group. Who owns the ideas that are generated? If you have invited friends round to help you generate ideas then it would be worth making sure that they are aware and agree that they will be helping you to come up with ideas to develop into real businesses. If they have a problem with this it may be best not to include them in the session unless you are considering them as business partners. For information on protecting ideas and confidentiality agreements read the later chapter: Protecting Your Idea. A certain degree of maturity is required here – everyone should agree that ideas will not be talked about outside of the group and that ideas remain the property of the person who came up with it unless they say otherwise (and I would recommend that if they do say this you get it in writing from them). Paranoid I may sound, but although your friend may be happy to give you an idea she has been sitting on for two years, she may not be so happy when you develop it into a multi million pound business and she sees nothing for it! The rule is to make sure everyone knows your intentions and what's going on!

The important thing to note about the Ideas Generation stage is that if you use the techniques and you come up with ideas that are *new and original to you* then they're working and you should carry on using them. Yes the idea may already have been made a reality by someone else but if it was the first time you had thought of it then the session has been successful – you have learned to make a new connection and been creative.

Being creative is merely a matter of conditioning your mind to make more and new connections on a regular basis. Most business ideas are either modifications of old ideas or old ideas brought into a new context. There is absolutely nothing wrong with this and the techniques outlined in this book thoroughly encourage it but every once in a while you may come up with something earth shatteringly new. If you use one or more of these techniques on a daily basis for ten minutes then you will after a couple of days notice an influx of new thinking and new ideas popping into your head.

Ideas Checker

This is the part of the process that many people feel they can miss out. I urge you not to do this. It is at this stage that we bring our critical faculties back and start to inspect and research the viability of our idea or ideas. This book will give you a series of questions you need to apply to your ideas to find out whether or not they are viable in the real world. I would caution you against basing your judgements on emotions but to follow the checklists provided. This part of the process can take anything from a couple of hours to a couple of days depending on the ideas you have come up with and the resources at your disposal. For those people who are already ideas people and constantly come up with new ideas the Ideas Checker will be invaluable. Often the problem these people have is sticking to one idea – they flit from idea to idea and rarely, if ever, achieve anything simply because they cannot make a decision. The tools provided in this book will help them to nail one idea down and get on with it.

    A prime example of this is a guy who I mentored who we shall call Jim. Jim was a twenty-one-year-old who had recently graduated from university. He was a hugely creative person who was constantly coming up with ideas. By the time I met him he had filled two small notepads with ideas and came up with several more during our initial meeting. It didn't take a genius to notice that most of these ideas were centred around his passion – football. Rather than show him the ideas generation techniques (for someone with such high creativity levels as Jim, ideas generation techniques would simply have made his problem worse) I went straight to the Ideas Checker processes. We applied it to one of his ideas and once I was sure he had the hang of it he went away and started to apply it to the three ideas that he liked the most. On carrying out the research he realised that two of them were potentially viable – one of them definitely wasn't. After more research and a further mentoring session, he identified the one idea that he wanted to take forward. We then developed an action plan based on the last part of the process to enable him to do this and make his idea a reality.

Ideas Implementation

You've come up with the idea, run it through the Ideas Checker and you're excited to find that its viable, has a good chance of being successful and you want to make it a reality. Although this book is primarily concerned with the first two parts of the process, in this section we will take a brief look at the steps you need to take to implement your idea. This includes whether or not you should have a business plan, what should be in it, the importance of mentors and support groups, marketing, networking and five questions that you really need to be able to answer. As mentioned in the Ideas Checker, Jim decided on the one idea he wanted to take forward. By sitting him down and giving him the tools detailed in the Ideas Implementation stage he was able to develop a simple business plan and perhaps more importantly, he was able to take stock of the resources and contacts he already had that could help him make his dream come true. The interesting thing is that if he had not gone through this process he would never have known what resources he had and would probably have missed them, which would have made implementation much more of a struggle for him.

Now that you know what creativity is, why you need it and you are aware of the ideas generation process, it's time to start looking at ideas and their sources.

THREE

SOURCES OF IDEAS

IN THIS CHAPTER YOU ARE going to learn where ideas come from. This is extremely important and something that is usually neglected in books on creative thinking. The four main sources that are used in this book are featured for very particular reasons, which make this book unique. Knowing these sources allows you to come up with ideas centred around you as a person. This means that your ideas will fascinate, excite and motivate you – all of which you will need when it comes to the implementation stage of the process.

Where do ideas come from? When you ask people this they give answers similar to those for creative thinking. Clichés such as "you spot a gap in the market" or "your dreams" or "your heart".

I contend that there are four main sources of ideas:

- Passions
- Hobbies
- Anger/Frustration
- Necessity

Passions

Passions are what makes life worth living. It is passion that adds juice to your life. It is what motivates an Olympic athlete to get up at five in the morning to run fifteen miles and then spend the rest of the day in a gruelling work out. Passion is what drives entrepreneurs such as Richard Branson, Donald Trump and Duncan Bannatyne. It may be passion for money, it may be a passionate need to beat the competition or it may simply be a passion for business, but without passion nothing great can be achieved and entrepreneurs would not have the energy or commitment to make their businesses and ideas work. So the question I have for you is: what is your passion? What fills your life with excitement and enables you to keep going when the going gets tough and all you want to do is hideaway and sleep? If you can state quite clearly and honestly what your passion is, then congratulations! That's fantastic. If you can't then answering these questions may help.

- Is there anything, which if taken away, would make your life meaningless?
- Is there something in your life, the very thought of which, fills you with excitement?
- Is there something you would be happy spending the rest of your life doing?
- Is there anything you do where you lose track of time and you find you are tired but happy?

I would recommend that if you haven't already done so, you read the autobiographies of anyone who has achieved anything tremendous – in this case famous entrepreneurs. They will quite clearly state what their passions are and you will be able to see how these passions have helped shape their success.

As with much of this system, passions are extremely personal – do not let yourself or anyone else be judgemental when stating yours. If your passion is your car or your cat or your garden, that's fantastic – as long as you are being honest, that is all that matters. The simple fact is, that whatever your passion, there will be someone else out there who shares it or at least has an interest in what you are passionate about. These people are your potential customers.

Hobbies

I often get asked the difference between hobbies and passions. The answer in my opinion is that whereas a passion *is* your life, hobbies are something that, although you really enjoy them on a regular basis and would miss them if they were taken away, if you were suddenly prevented from doing them your life would carry on as normal. Again as with passions there can be no judgement. If your hobby is watching episodes of *Star Trek* or lurking on internet forums then that's great. There are bound to be people who share the same hobby as you. Hobbies usually make people congregate and communicate and these people are potential customers for you. You may well have more than one hobby and that's fine as well.

Anger/Frustration

In my experience this is the one that nobody has a problem with. Everyone has at least one thing (usually seven) that annoys and frustrates the hell out of them. It could be anything – from queuing for food, to rude and ignorant people, to speeding drivers. Whatever it is, if it annoys you, you can guarantee that it also annoys other people and these people are potential customers. I would argue that if something frustrates you or makes you angry then it's because the current strategy you are using to handle it isn't working – anger and frustration are your mind and body's way of telling you that you need to be more creative in the way you approach things. One example of someone having set-up a business based on something that annoys him is a man who complains for people; if you have suffered from poor customer service then you can pay him to write letters of complaint to the organisation, often resulting in an apology and freebies.

Necessity

Shelter, oxygen, food, and water – these are absolute necessities for sustaining human life. It's amazing how many people now consider the internet to be vital to them, along with their iPods, mobile phones and so on. Again no judgements are to be made. If you consider something to be necessary to your survival then it is necessary. If you can come up with a business idea that ties in with a human necessity then you have the potential to be very successful. As the human race is, arguably, an addictive race, this includes such things as sex and drugs. These businesses are not always legal but they are a clear example of the fact. Connected to this are those items/products/services that humans need to use again and again – a brilliant example of this is disposable razor blades.

So now that you now where ideas come from we are going to plunge into the creative techniques and learn one that uses all of the above, is extremely powerful and is guaranteed to have you coming up with new ideas within thirty-minutes or less.

BRILLIANT BUSINESS IDEAS

FOUR

THE IDEAS MATRIX

THE IDEAS MATRIX IS ONE of my favourite techniques because it brings together everything you have read previously, and is both extremely simple and powerful. It is the very essence of creativity. Many people I have worked with rely on this one technique alone. It is so versatile that an entire book could be written it and we will be coming back to it in later chapters when we look at making employees more creative. In this chapter you are going to learn the fundamentals, look at examples of where it has been used to generate a business idea and then carry out an exercise to make sure you understand the technique and that it works for you. You can use this technique for anything from planning a novel to designing a marketing campaign but for this book we will be using it in a business context.

Take a look at this chart:

Passion	Hobby	Anger or Frustration	Necessity

As you can see we have the four sources of ideas in a table.

You can either do this technique exercise on your own or in a group. What I want you to do is start putting in the things you are passionate about into the Passion column, detailing your hobbies in the Hobbies column, noting the things that frustrate or anger you in the Anger/Frustration column and write down the things you consider necessary to your survival into the Necessity column. If you are in a group, take it in turns and end up with entries in each column from everybody, all listed in the same chart.

THE IDEAS MATRIX

Once you have finished your chart should look something along these lines:

Passion	Hobby	Anger or Frustration	Necessity
Martial Arts	Graphic Design	Rude People	Shelter
Web Design	Piano	Dangerous Drivers	Good food
Music	Walking	Bad novels	Water
Sexy cars	Dancing	Studying	Love
		Essay writing	Air
			Internet
			Television

Remember what creativity is all about? Making connections. We're going to start to make connections between the words in the columns. The connections can be with words in the same column, the one next to it or the one on the far side – it really doesn't matter as long as the connections are being made. The connections you make should be in a business context.

For example:

Passion	Hobby	Anger or Frustration	Necessity
Martial Arts	Graphic Design	Rude People	Shelter
Web Design	Piano	Dangerous Drivers	Good food
Music	Walking	Bad novels	Water
Sexy cars	Dancing	Studying	Love
		Essay writing	

We have made connections between the following – web design, music and walking. How could we link these words or activities in a business context? At this moment remember we are merely looking for ideas. The judging of those ideas will come later on – at the moment we need to focus on getting a good crop of them to analyse and judge. So to start with how about an online business that organises walks for people in the Lake District where each person is equipped with an iPod and can listen to specific music and poetry inspired by the scenery? Rubbish? Bizarre? Maybe but it's one new idea that we did not have previously, which means that we are making new connections and therefore this technique is working for us. Every member of the group should be making his or her own connections and noting them down. Focus on making as many connections as you can and don't stop to think about whether or not they are ridiculous. A teenage group session came up with the idea of using your mobile phone to pay for products in a shop when there are huge queues. There would be a telephone number you could call, every product would have a serial number and by following the instructions on your phone and paying by card, the product would be yours. This would cut down on queues – especially during peak times such as summer and Christmas sales. I believe that some retail chains have started doing this fairly recently but the first time I heard about it was from this group. By taking something that most people now consider necessary to their survival (the mobile phone) and linking it up to something that a lot of people enjoy (shopping) and linking that up to something that angers many people (queues) this group came up with quite an original idea.

You can either start purposefully to make connections or nominate one of the group members to start picking out words and columns at random and then the rest of the group has to make connections (all of which must be in a business context). I prefer to purposefully make connections but if I'm working with a group which is a little slow to get started and their imaginations need a quick workout, then I will pick out words at random and they will have to make connections.

Exercise

Fill in the blank table and take ten-minutes to make some connections and see what happens. You will be surprised at how many connections you can make – some of them will seem bizarre, others will obviously never work but there will be one or two that will definitely be worthy of further investigation.

Passion	Hobby	Anger or Frustration	Necessity

Case Study

Jenny was twenty-one and had one term left at university before she graduated with a degree in marketing. She had been involved in a number of activities, clubs and societies and she now wanted to set-up her own business. She had a number of ideas, none of which she was particularly attached to, which suggested to me that those ideas weren't right for her. After an initial chat I decided to use the Ideas Matrix with her. By the way, in case you haven't already guessed – this technique allows you to find a lot out about a person. I got her to draw the chart and then started interrogating her about her passions, her hobbies and so on. I've written the dialogue below to show you how a session works and to show how, through the use of questions (which we shall discuss in a later chapter) I get the information out of people.

J: OK Jenny, so what are you passions?

Jen: (laughs) Oh God – I don't know really…

J: Well what do you really enjoy? What gives your life juice? What gets you really worked up?

Jen: Well I really like sports – I'm into athletics and keeping fit. I like meeting up with my friends and I like going to the cinema with them…

J: Right – just eh – let me note all these down. So your passions; you're telling me your passions are sport – especially athletics and socialising with friends?"

Jen: Yep.

J: Good stuff. We'll get more specific later on but for now let's just get something in each column. Now what about your hobbies – those things that you do on a regular basis but if truth be told you could do without. You enjoy them and you would miss them but they wouldn't alter your life at all if they disappeared.

Jen: OK...well...I guess reading would be a hobby, crime novels. I enjoy cooking – especially for family and friends. If I'm in the mood then I enjoy shopping. I also do some voluntary work with young school children which I really enjoy – I do a few hours a week.

J: And onto things that get you angry or frustrate you. What gets you really annoyed? What things frustrate the hell out of you?

Jen: Bad attitudes in sport really make me angry. Lazy people and rude people. Bad customer service really annoys me especially in restaurants when the waiters are rude or pretend to ignore you. Oh and bad drivers – especially dangerous drivers. My little brother (laughs). *Note how in common with everyone else I know Jen knows exactly what frustrates her and makes her angry.*

J: Ok I think we have enough there. Now what things do you consider necessary to your survival. And yes you can and should include such things as water, shelter, air and food.

Jen: This sounds really silly...

J: No it doesn't go on...

Jen: Well I would go crazy without my iPod and if I didn't have the internet I would be lost. Obviously all the things you said as well – food, shelter, water, love and oxygen.

J: Excellent. What we're going to do now is go back over things and be a little bit more specific ok. So first of all Passions. You mentioned sports and athletics. I know you were a member of a number of student sports clubs but which one do you enjoy the most.

Jen: No contest – it would have to be cheerleading. I was President of the cheerleading team last year and we got through to national competitions.

J: Wow! So you were very good at cheerleading and a very good President. That's interesting. And you're really passionate about cheerleading are you?

Jen: *Her eyes light up at the thought of cheerleading and I can tell that her excitement is genuine.* Yes absolutely! In fact I would have liked another shot at President but I had to give it up to study for my final year. I'm still on the team as a cheerleader.

J: You listed another passion as socialising with your friends.

Jen: Yeah.

J: But would you say that cheerleading is your main passion?

Jen: Thinking about it – yes I guess so. Yep.

J: So I'm thinking a business that is cheerleading related would be right down your street?

Jen: Yes but I'm not certain how you would do that. If

we were in America it would be easy because cheerleading is big business. *Jen is starting to make judgements about a potential business idea which I don't want her to do at this stage as such judgement without research can kill off what may be a very viable idea. By now I have a few ideas of what Jen could do but I am anxious not to impose my ideas onto her – I have made a note of them just in case she has difficulty in making connections before our session ends, but not shown her.*

J: Well let's not consider what's viable and what's not at the moment. Let's just concentrate on coming up with ideas. So we've identified that cheerleading is an area that would be exciting for you to be involved in, in a business context. Let's leave that here for now and get more specific with your hobbies. You said that you enjoy reading, in particular crime novels. You also enjoy shopping – shopping for what exactly? Food? Clothes? Or is it just shopping?

Jen: *Laughing.* Clothes in the main or presents for other people.

J: So how could we link up your like of shopping with cheerleading? Are there suppliers of cheerleading uniforms?

Jen: Pulls a face. There are a few companies in the UK that offer specialist cheerleading wear. To be honest, it's not something I'm that into and also I hate pom-poms so...

J: OK I can see that that's not the idea for you. Tell me more about the voluntary work you do with young children.

Jen: Well I go into schools on a volunteer project and help primary and secondary school children with their basic reading skills. I go in for maybe half a day a week.

J: Do you really enjoy this or is it something you do for your CV? Which isn't a problem but if you do enjoy it then I think it's something we should look at a bit closer.

Jen: No I really do enjoy it. It can be both frustrating and very satisfying. It's the one thing besides the cheerleading that I have kept up in my final year.

She pauses then says: I wonder – do you think a cheerleading club for young children would work?"
I already had this idea noted down.

J: Well let's not worry about that for a moment – we'll have a look at that later on. Does the idea of running your own cheerleading club sound good to you?

Jen: Yeah! In fact I don't know why I didn't think of it before. I know there's a club in my hometown which is very successful and I know for a fact that cheerleading is one of the fastest growing sports in the UK.

Having found an idea that Jen found exciting and wanted to investigate further we ended the session ten-minutes early and I took her through the Ideas Checker part of the process so she could check out the viability of the idea. What's interesting about this session is that I could see the idea Jen came up with fairly early on in the session but it took her a little longer to figure it out. This is often the case and what may seem obvious to the observer is not so obvious to the person who is filling in the table. If you do use this technique on your own it would be worth getting someone to have a look at your completed matrix and the connections you have made to see if you have missed any fairly obvious ones. Note also that I prevent Jen and re-focus her when she is in danger of making a judgement – if you're doing this in a group then keep an eye on each other and if you're on your own have the discipline to merely note the ideas down. Judgement will come later.

Jen's completed Ideas Matrix looked like this:

Passion	Hobby	Anger or Frustration	Necessity
Socialising with friends	Reading crime novels	Rude People	iPod
Sports, athletics, cheerleading	Volunteering with young children	Bad attitudes in sport	Internet
		Lazy people	Air
		Dangerous drivers	Water
			Food
			Shelter

She went through the entire process outlined in this book, proved to her own satisfaction that her idea was viable and likely to be successful and went on to set-up her own club. Early on she was offered investment but turned it down as she was confident that she could do it by herself.

More Case Studies

Liz is a secondary school teacher who specialises in special needs. On her weekends she also works with blind children taking them on trips and helping them to have new experiences. She was looking for a business idea or product that she could do outside of her main job. When she came to see me it was very simple to list her passions and hobbies – they were all centred around teaching and working with blind children. Her frustrations were around the public's perceptions of her students and the young people she worked with. We spent some time discussing these. One of the things that really irritated her was that toys were often brightly coloured – especially for the younger children. While she knew that children liked colour and the toys were suitable for blind children she felt they deserved toys just for them. Within fifteen minutes she had come up with the idea of a jigsaw for blind children. One that would feel different would smell lots of smells and make sounds. Off the back of this she came up with a few more ideas. Within half an hour she had an entire product range of toys for blind children. She is currently researching these ideas further and looking into the possibility of having them manufactured. There are, she knows, similar products on the market but she believes that some of her ideas are truly innovative and would not cost too much.

Barry is a keen gardener. "Actually, past tense is more correct," he admits "I was a keen gardener but since moving to London there's no real space for me to do any gardening and I certainly can't afford a house with a garden or a plot of land." While he loved the city and the hectic social life that it allowed him his one big frustration was that he couldn't do any gardening.

"I found it really relaxing and its actually really satisfying. Some people do jogging or tai chi – I do gardening." By making the connection between something he really enjoyed (he couldn't quite make up his mind as to whether gardening was a passion or a hobby) and his frustration –the lack of space for a garden – he came up with the idea of roof top herb gardens.

"I know for a fact that there's nothing new in this but my little brother recently went to university. I went to visit him and he had a very dull room which he had done up with posters but there were no plants there. I thought that I might specialise in window-sill herb gardens and just plain window-sill gardens for students." He's already started his research to find out if this idea is viable or not.

"One good thing that has become really apparent is that students and young people are much more conscious than we thought about their health and the environment. It's also actually pretty trendy for people to grow their own food and some universities are actually encouraging it. It's looking promising."

Someone who came up with another environment (or green) linked business idea is Julie. Julie was a housewife whose children had both left home. Her husband worked a lot of the time and she wanted an idea for a part-time business. She couldn't think of any passions so we went on to hobbies. I couldn't help noticing that most of her hobbies were to do with improving the environment, she was part of a recycling committee on the local council, and she had spearheaded a number of green issues in her local area. It took us less than ten-minutes to work out that the environment was a passion. One of her hobbies was cleaning, which she was a bit bashful about.

"I know it's a bit boring but I find it relaxing to clean a house from top to bottom. I actually feel better once it's been done and the house feels all fresh." I asked her how she could link up her passion for green issues with her hobby for cleaning. She thought for a few moments then her eyes lit up. "I could offer a house cleaning service that only uses environmentally friendly products." Julie is currently looking into this and has found herself a supplier of green products which are promised to work better than the mainstream equivalents.

You will see in this chapter that I asked a number of questions. In the next chapter we are going to look at the power of asking questions and what happens when you apply them in a business context. Do you realise the power of asking intelligent questions?

BRILLIANT BUSINESS IDEAS

FIVE

AWKWARD QUESTIONS

ARE YOU A PARENT? DO you baby-sit for friends at all? Do you have any young nieces or nephews? Are you a primary school teacher? If you are any of the above or you have any contact with young children at all then you will know that they ask a massive number of questions. In fact, research apparently shows that the average four-year-old child can ask up to 437 questions a day! Why do they ask this many questions? Quite simply because their brains are constantly trying to make new connections, and because they don't yet have all the knowledge which they expect the adults to supply to them. To children everything around them is new – they're not at the stage where they have enough experience to make any assumptions of which all adults are guilty. This is why they are constantly learning and they learn by asking questions. Next time a child asks you a question you may want to consider your answer and not give them a glib response.

Most adults stop asking so many questions – they certainly won't ask as many as 437 questions a day and most of the questions they do ask won't be as intelligent or thoughtful as those asked by four-year-olds.

Children aren't the only ones that ask lots of

questions. Entrepreneurs and creative people, in my experience, do three things:

- They ask questions.
- They don't stop asking questions until they get what they want.
- They act on the answers they receive (we will be looking at taking action in the implementation stage of the ideas process)

Don't underestimate the power of questions. Questions have changed the course of history for both good and bad. People such as Ghandi and Hitler are two perfect examples. The suffragette movement which won women the vote in the UK started because women asked a question; why shouldn't they have the vote? A small group of women started to ask that question in a very forceful public way, turned it round into a statement and eventually won women the right to vote. Most entrepreneurs have the same talent for asking questions and acting on the answers they get to create momentum.

Think about it – before you can take action of any kind or make a decision you have to ask a question – even if it's only to yourself.

In this chapter you will learn the following principle:

If you ask an intelligent question you will get an intelligent answer

This may sound simple but think about how it impacts massively upon your life. If you spend most of your time asking questions such as: "Why does it always happen to me? Why can I never get a break?", can you imagine the sort of answers and excuses you will get from your mind and the world around you?

Imagine, though, deciding instead to ask this type of question: "What actions can I take to ensure that this never happens again?" or "What do I need to do to ensure that I have XX in my life?"

All of a sudden you are asking intelligent questions to which you will receive intelligent answers. Why? Because you have moved your focus from poor quality to proactive and focused questions. It's very similar to the well-known saying of computer programmers, that if you put crap in, you get crap out.

Our heading of Awkward Questions, then, is merely a list of questions that you can apply to anything you want, so that you generate new ideas for products and businesses. They are called awkward because, believe it or not, although there is nothing particularly special about them, most people don't ask them – they simply accept things as they are and get on with things. Rintu Basu, a great NLP Trainer who has spent most of his life asking questions, formulated the questions with me.

There is only one rule with this technique: *You must carry on asking the questions until you are supplied with an answer you are happy with.*

You will know when you're on the right track when people start to avoid you because you ask too many questions!

Here are the questions, which I have divided into different categories for ease of use:

How Questions

- **How does it work?** This doesn't have to be technical – you could apply this question to the behaviour of animals or humans. By knowing how something works you will be able to spot inefficiencies and things that could be improved.

- **How could we improve this?** This is one question that you should constantly be asking yourself and the people with whom you work. Even when your business is set-up and running smoothly, make sure you never stop asking this question. The Japanese have a work philosophy called *Kaizen* which roughly translated means "Constant and never ending improvement". This is also a question we will be focusing on in the chapter on Negative Thinking.

- **How could I make this better?** It is amazing how many people spend years or even decades in a job and don't ask themselves this question. They merely trudge into work and continue to do what they have always done the way they were taught. By asking this question you are seeking to add value not only to your role but to yourself.

- **How could I do this cheaper?** This is an especially good question to ask if you want to add value to the company for which you work or save your own business some money. I used to be a buyer for a large company and it was amazing how many of my colleagues had stopped asking this question. This is also a great question to ask in your personal life – particularly in the current economic situation.

Why Questions

- **Why do we do it like that?** The first answer to this question will often be: Because we have always done it like that! If this is the first answer you get then keep on asking the question as there is a good chance that there is room for improvement or innovation.

- **Why do we have to do it?** This is one of my favourites. I focused on this one when working with some secondary school children. At the end of the workshop one boy approached his teacher and asked why he had to do his homework. Before she could answer he went onto say that he didn't enjoy doing it and he suspected that she didn't enjoy having to read and mark it so wouldn't everyone be much happier if he just didn't do it? I had to laugh and really admired the boy's ability to negotiate. His teacher although highly amused (and I suspect highly impressed) remained firm – he would have to continue doing his homework. I have a feeling that this boy will be a fantastic salesmen when he is older.

- **Why does it work that way?** Inherent in this question is an assumption that there are other ways something could work. Also, by knowing why something works the way it does it suddenly becomes much easier to pinpoint the things that need to change to get a different result.

Where Questions

- **Where else do we see these patterns/this process?** Have you come across a product or business that serves a particular need that is very similar to a second need? Can you transfer the idea to meet the second need? We will be looking at this more in the Ideas Heist chapter.

- **Where else do we see this problem/issue?** Can you find a similar problem in an entirely different context? How was it solved? Can you apply the solution to your problem or issue? This is another question that is an entire creative thinking technique in itself – that of metaphors, which we don't look at too much in this book but is on the website.

What Questions

- **What should we do?** This can be a very powerful question – notice it's not what we can do but what should we do. Asking this with regard to an area such as customer service could prove to be very interesting.

- **What is wrong with this?** You can always find something wrong if you look hard enough. We will be focusing on this question in the chapter on Negative Thinking.

- **What needs to be put right about this?** The inherent assumption that something is wrong in the first place is a powerful one to make that may lead you to notice faults previously not apparent to you.

- **What if we didn't do it at all?** Depending on the context, you can really shock people by asking this question but it is one worth asking. Provided that it wouldn't be dangerous or hurt anyone then this question can really add value.

- **What would happen if?** By exploring various alternative scenarios you start to create new avenues to explore which potentially could lead to new ideas.

- **What else could I apply this to?** Very often ideas can be applied in more than one context. Some of the most successful products and business ideas originally had a very different end-use in mind when first created. This is actually an entire creative technique in itself! Whoever came up with the idea of adding a camera to the mobile phone? Stop and think about it for a moment. It really is a bizarre idea on the face of it yet it worked.

- **What doesn't happen when we do this?** Similar to "What would happen if?" You might want to also ask "Does it matter if this doesn't happen?"

- **What purpose does this service?** This is a vital question because what it's really asking is what gap or need in the market are you fulfilling and is there really a need for what you are offering? We will be looking at this in much more detail in the Idea Checker chapter.

- **For what purpose are we doing this?** So often people forget why they are doing something. I often think that creative thinking sessions fall prey to this as people get caught up with their ideas. By asking this question and asking it often you will ensure that you stick to your objectives.

- **For what purpose would we want to do it differently?** We often get stuck and do things the way we've done them because we've always done them that way. By asking this question and exploring scenarios that would change our processes we start to get a fresh perspective on them. This can lead to useful ideas we can use in the current context.

- **What are the steps to get the results I want?** Often a task or objective may seem impossible to reach. By asking this question and breaking things down into steps you automatically start creating a map or process. These mini steps make the required result easier to obtain and also allow us to inspect each step in detail and decide whether or not it is really necessary.

- **What's not possible?** Very often the obstacles in our paths are assumed. They don't always exist and it's the same in business. By asking this question you will start to strip away all the false obstacles.

- **What purpose do they serve?** A great question for getting rid of the unnecessary and speeding things up or saving money. This question also allows you to put things into their proper place and gain a better understanding of the whole picture.

Miscellaneous Questions

- **Wouldn't it be better if we did it like this?** Don't be scared to try out a number of scenarios – this is a good one to couple with the one above it.

- **Which of those steps can we leave out?** Can you come up with a business idea that can deliver things to people faster or provide a faster service in some way? Is there a business market you want to move into that is already full? Can you spot a flaw in their business processes that would give you an edge?

- **Which of those steps can we combine/ change/modify?** This is connected to the above question and will aid in speeding things up, saving money, and improving things.

- **Do they really want that?** Just because people buy something it doesn't mean that they actually want it. It may well be the only thing they can get – don't automatically assume that because everyone buys something its a quality product or any good. It may mean that there's an opportunity and gap in the market.

- **Does it need to be that good?** Having worked with engineers I know for a fact that given freedom they would always want the highest quality piece of equipment when in actual fact a lower quality piece of equipment would suffice. Be careful of the six-hundred dollar toilet seat scenario (although an urban legend, the term refers to the time when a contractor charged the government an extravagant amount of money for toilet seat covers. It is now used to refer to large wastes of money.)

- **Is that a fact or an assumption?** It's amazing how much the business world, even with its emphasis on market research, still makes a massive number of assumptions. When someone tells you that something won't work because "everyone knows" or "the research shows" it may well be worth being awkward and checking it out for yourself.

These are good questions to apply to anything that makes you angry or gets you frustrated. They're also good for product development or product improvement. Some of them may seem to be repeated but they are all subtly different and if asked should therefore provide slightly different answers.

Case Study

Martha was a journalist for a local newspaper. When she came to see me she was depressed.

"I've just quit my job," she announced "so I need to come up with an idea quick!" This is never the best way to do it, but I sat her down and asked her the obvious question: Why are you depressed?

"I rang the police yesterday morning as I always do to see if any potential stories had occurred overnight. The policeman who answered the phone told me there had been a massive car accident with two people dead and a large number of people seriously injured." At this point she looked down ashamed. "My first thought was 'what a great story this would be' and I suddenly hated myself and the job I was doing."

We chatted a bit more then. "So you don't like your job because all anyone seems to want to hear is bad news?"

"Basically yes. I'm not sure that people do want to read bad news all the time though. I mean look at the media these days and its all bad news! I have so many friends who have stopped reading newspapers and watching the news because they are sick of all the negativity." It was very obvious that Martha asked herself and the people around her a lot of questions (she was a journalist after all).

"What would happen," I asked her "if you started writing good-news stories?" She thought for a moment.

"I don't know…I mean I don't want to see the world through rose-tinted glasses – I just want acknowledgement that good things do happen, that people can be good to each other." She looked at me and asked with excitement: "Why isn't there a newspaper that highlights all the good stuff that goes on?"

"I don't know" I replied.

"Well I'm damn well going to find out" she told me. Feeling much better she left to start her research into the possibilities.

One of the most common questions that entrepreneurs seem to ask themselves is:

How can I make more money with no risk to myself and with only very little use of my time and energy? Miguel (more of whom later on) asked this question and came up with a whole counter-top of new products that he could sell to his customers. Someone else made them, he got them on sale-or-return and he took a percentage of sales. Another entrepreneur who does this has managed to double his income in one area of his business – ironically the one into which he puts the least amount of work.

Exercise

What makes you angry or frustrated? You should already have some answers close to hand if you have completed the Ideas Matrix exercise. It doesn't matter what you wrote in the column, spend ten-minutes applying a few of the questions from the list to your points and see if you get any answers worth following up. I remember doing this exercise with some school children. We decided that we would apply the questions to things that annoy and frustrate me. One of the things that really annoys me is getting stuck behind people who walk slowly while I'm shopping. This seems to happen to me whenever I'm in a shop and it really irritates me as I'm a fast walker and I want to get my shopping done so I can get home quickly. The school children thought this was funny so we applied the questions to it and some of the answers they came up with were hilarious (though often illegal). One that stuck in my mind as being very clever was to put fast music on the shop speakers to make people move faster. What a fantastic idea! Would it work? I believe so. OK it's not a business idea but it's a clever answer and we would never have got it if we hadn't asked an intelligent question. Get asking questions and see what you come up with.

Second Exercise

One of the funny things about human beings is that we are creatures of habit. Most of us are so conditioned that we unthinkingly walk through life. Look out for signs and start making a habit of asking questions. Questions about your daily working habits, the way you travel to work, why the people around you behave as they do. I want you to develop a questioning attitude because by asking questions you are becoming more aware. The answers you get probably won't lead to business ideas but it's vital that you get into the habit of asking questions. I once did a creative thinking workshop for senior citizens and, although I had no proof, I shared with them my belief that by striving to make new connections and by practicing these techniques they could stave off the decline of mental faculties connected with old age. When I declared my belief in the importance of asking questions one elderly gentlemen stood up and volunteered that he had a habit of asking questions because his father had taught him to do so. His father never stopped asking questions and according to this man lived a very full and rich life – it was clear that this man believed that this was largely due to his father's attitude and need to ask questions.

Another exercise would be to formulate your own questions. I've given you some very general questions – can you come up with more specific examples for particular situations in which you may find yourself?

SIX

THE IDEAS HEIST

ENTREPRENEURS AREN'T ALWAYS THE MOST original of people. They may not come up with original innovative ideas all the time but what they may well do is take an idea and transfer it to a totally different context. Every day around the world people are coming up with and trying out new ideas. The truth is that as long as you're prepared to do your research there are plenty of ideas out there just waiting to be slightly changed or implemented and made a reality. I call this technique the Ideas Heist because that is essentially what you are doing. Now I'm not advocating the theft of an idea or doing something illegal. I'm suggesting that you look long and hard at the ideas that are popping up every day and find ways to apply them or change them and make them your own. Obviously if someone has a patent or has protected their idea then there is little you can do but there are a lot of ideas out there that you can't actually protect. Anthony Robbins in his book Unlimited Power talks about a very similar thing. He points out that if someone is making a lot of money in one country by having birthday cakes delivered by people wearing silly fancy dress costumes, then the chances are you can have a similar success in your country before the original business expands to your area. He calls the time it takes for a business to expand lag time. Most of us have access to the internet. Use it and start looking at business ideas that are successful in other countries. One website and newsletter I cannot recommend highly enough is www.springwise.com. This is a website that shows off the latest business ideas from around the world with a few comments on their current success and viability. There is also a monthly newsletter that I recommend you sign up for. The range and quality of ideas reported is astounding and very inspiring – definitely worth a look. Very often the most transferable ideas will be those that offer a service though not always. Once you've found an idea that you like, you need to make sure that is not protected.

You also need to check whether or not that business was set-up to suit a particular culture or religious need. What you are really looking at is the compatibility and transferability of the idea. If you suspect that it is successful in one country or region because it caters for a particularly unique aspect of that region or country then is there anything you can change about it to suit your own? Crepes are a popular food in France and America but not so much in the UK. Two young men decided to change that and opened up their own crêperie which became highly successful. The toppings and fillings that they offer their customers are extremely different from those offered in France.

You may also want to take note of the way the idea

or business has been marketed – would these methods work in your country?

Miguel, who we met in the introduction, was a third-year politics student. Before university he had worked in London's Canary Wharf selling and serving soup for a company. He would attract the attention of the bankers and stock brokers with the cry of "hot soup hot soup". When he went North to university he was shocked by how bad the weather was and how cold it got in the winter. He was also astounded by the complete lack of cafes serving healthy food. A self declared foodie he was always making casseroles and stews and the lads he lived with started to notice. Soon he was cooking for the entire house and this was when he started asking himself questions. On campus there was no shop or cafe he could find that served quality hot winter foods such as soup. He asked himself why he couldn't offer students healthy and fantastic tasting soup. Having asked that question he got a simple answer – he could! He started to make soup and by asking more questions he found out who he needed to talk to about getting space on the campus and permission to actually sell his soup. It took a lot of work and energy but he now has an outlet where he sells food that is famous on campus and has a large number of regular customers. Once he had got this, Miguel carried on asking questions. What other foods could he offer to his customers? What other things could he offer that would take up little to no amount of his time energy or money? He started offering vegetarian chilli and jams and marmalades made on farms on the local area. These increased his sales and required very little energy or money. Miguel carries on running his successful business and continues to ask questions. His idea is not particularly original but with it having worked in London Miguel had a fair idea that it would work on a campus based university.

Start looking at the businesses around you. How many successful examples of idea heists can you find? The fast food industry for one is full of them. Look at online businesses – everywhere you will find ideas that have been picked up by someone and set-up in a new location or ideas that have been changed slightly but are just as successful and sometimes more successful than the original. Look at the multitude of smoothies that have appeared on our supermarket shelves since Innocent came along and raised the smoothie profile as a healthy ethical drink.

Exercise

Visit the springwise.com website and sign up for the newsletter. Check the ideas that are featured on the website and see if any of them appeal to you. Some of my favourites include a business that offers one-off unique lingerie to the highest bidder, a wine cellar that can be installed in any home and a website that allows you to design your own chocolate bar, have it made and delivered to your home. If any of them do appeal to you then go straight onto the Ideas Checker and run them through it. Remember, however, if the idea is protected in some way (most of them have a website and it will tell you there) then you will have to leave it and look elsewhere.

Second Exercise

Have a look in the business sections of newspapers (often Sunday newspapers have a business or small business supplement). There will be case studies of start-up businesses in the UK and abroad. Are there any that capture your interest? Start making a list of them and keeping the cuttings. Are there any that you can take, change slightly and make your own?

In the next chapter we're going to look at the power of Negative Thinking. When it comes to business ideas generation, negative thinking can be much more powerful than positive thinking.

SEVEN

NEGATIVE THINKING

THIS IS ONE TECHNIQUE THAT lots of people will find easy and which is extremely useful for improving a product (your own or a competitors) or, like awkward questions, applying it to situations that annoy and frustrate you. Basically take something and start making statements about all the things you really dislike about it – they can be as extreme and as silly as you want – we will filter the statements later on. What you end up with is a blueprint for things that could be improved. Reversing those things you have a list of things that you might actually like and hey presto a new product. This is another good technique to do in a group as other people will spot negative things that you have missed. If you know someone who always finds the problem then team up with them for this exercise as they have already trained their minds to think in this way. Things to focus on when thinking negatively include:

- **Shape**. Is the shape unattractive? Is it awkward to hold, awkward to put into a space or on a shelf? Take a look at the hundreds of different shaped containers and products on your local supermarket shelf. One company who spends a lot of time considering shape is Dyson – look at their range of vacuum cleaners!

- **Size.** Is it too big or too small? What would be the ideal size? Often this is more about the customers perception than any practical consideration. If a customer spends a lot of money then often big is better. However, one area in which this is not true is technology, such as the rise of small-form computers (Mac minis for example) and ever smaller mobile phones.

- **Speed.** Too fast? Too slow? What would be the ideal speed? With technology usually the faster the better. We live in a world that considers speed to be better.

- **Weight.** Too heavy? Too light? As with the size issue, this can be a reflection of the customer's perception.

- **Durability.** Does it wear too quickly or is it durable and long lasting? How long does it need to last for?

- **Number of applications.** Is the product or service you're looking at only for one thing? Or can it be used in multiple contexts? Is the business missing out on a trick?

- **Smell.** This may seem slightly odd but the human sense of smell is extremely powerful and important hence the production of all the products to make your personal living space smell nice. Could the smell of the product be improved? Would any smell at all make the product better? The old trick of making coffee and baking bread when you're having people round to view your house works on a similar principle.

- **Availability.** How available is the product? A lot of business books are talking about exclusivity these days. Internet businesses, particularly those with the information products, tend to limit the number they sell and the date by which they will sell them. People want what they can't have or what few people have. However it may be that the product needs a large number of customers. Whichever it is, is there a clear and direct route to getting it? Often the shops run out of the most popular children's presents at Christmas. While this may be deliberate to keep demand high it could also be down to bad planning and poor supply chains.

- **Popularity.** How popular is the product/service you are looking at? Could it be more popular or is it universally loved and admired?

This is a huge one to consider if you are thinking about moving into a market that already has players in it – we shall look at this more in the Checker stage of the book. If the current players in the market are dominating it then it may be wiser to look elsewhere.

- **Lifetime.** How long is the product/service supposed to last for? And does it last this long in the real world?

- **Ease of use.** Is the product or service easy to use? Or is it highly complex? If so will someone help out the customer or is there a clear instruction manual with the service/product?

- **Feeling.** If you're looking at a product does it feel right? Someone once came to me with environmentally friendly bags. They were great – durable and well made and you could have any design on them in any colour you want. As the primary customers were going to be females we gave a few out to girls in their late teens to try out for a week. When they came back they all said the same thing – the bags felt rough on their skin and irritated their hands and made them uncomfortable. It is unlikely that these bags would get used for long or be recommended so for this guy it was back to the drawing board.

- **Effectiveness.** How good is the product at its primary job/function. For example there are plenty of car vacuum cleaners out there but I'm damned if I can find one that has any real suction power. Yet people still buy them. Could you vastly increase the suction power of a car vacuum cleaner? If so then I'll be your first customer!

- **Extras.** Does the product come with any extras? If you check out information products on the internet or watch the late-night cable shopping channels you will see there are often a number of bonus materials added when you purchase a product. A value is attached to these and if the customer feels he is getting more "bang for his buck" then he will be happy. Alternatively, are there any extras that the product should come with but doesn't? Are there any extras you could add that would increase not only the perceived value of the product but also its usefulness?

- **Colour.** Is the product the right colour? Cars used to come in limited colours but now there is a dazzling array out there from gun-metal grey to bright gold yellow. A colour can impact upon a potential customers perception. For example would you buy a car that is green with pink spots (then again some people would) – it's a matter of taste.

- **Sound.** If the product makes a sound does it make the right sound? Does the sound make it sexy? Can you improve upon it in some way? A good example to think about would be a motorbike. It can look big and sexy but if it sounds wimpy then a lot of people will be put off.

- **Cost.** How much does the product cost? One lady who made hand bags cheaply found that her sales went through the roof when she started selling them at incredibly high prices. Celebrities and the girl friends of male celebrities started buying them and before she knew it she had a designer product on her hands with huge profit margins.

- **Aftercare.** Does the product or service come with any aftercare? These days most purchases including services come with a warranty and a guarantee. Is there anything else that is offered or could be offered to make it more attractive to the customer?

If you're looking at a service then some other things to consider are:

- **Customer service.** Is there a high level of customer service? Are the staff knowledgeable about their products and do they treat you with respect? This stands as much for one-man bands as it does for High Street chains. Some of the most impressive people are those in mobile phone shops – the amount of knowledge they need is tremendous.

- **Extras.** Are there any extras offered? One garage close to where I live offered me a coffee while they fixed my car. It may seem like a small thing and would come under customer service but it exceeded my expectations and I'll make a point of going back to them again. What are the current service providers not doing that you could?

- **Premises.** Are the premises in a good location. Are they clean and welcoming? Are they too hot or too cold? Are the toilets clean? Are they easy to find? Are the premises highly visible?

Once you've gone through the list and torn the product or service apart (remember you can be as extreme and as silly as you want) its then time to sit down and start evaluating what you've got. If you've used negative thinking properly then you should have quite a few things that could greatly improve a product or service.

Case Study: Robin

When applying negative thinking to something you can be as detailed as you want to be. Someone who applied it to almost obsessive levels is Robin. Robin is a board game enthusiast. Not only are board games his hobby, they are also his passion so it was natural that his ideas would be centred around them. He had invented a number of board games which he would play with his family. *Total Strategy* came about because he felt that many games were not as well thought-out as they could be and that they had so much more potential. He wanted to create a game that had no bad points or faults; a board game that could be simple or complicated, modified, stripped down and have endless possibilities. He made a strategy game that can be customised by players, is based on one simple mechanic that is easy to learn and is suitable for all skill levels and age groups. Since 2004 Robin has developed *Total Strategy* so that there are a number of different branches.

"I felt there was a gap in the market. There were some classic strategy games such as chess and *Risk*. There were also warfare games using models that were more of a lifestyle than a board game, with all the model painting, creation of landscapes and so on. But otherwise, there seemed to be nothing decent available. My game *Total Strategy* is situated between *Risk* and the warfare games which is quite a big gap."

NEGATIVE THINKING

Robin applied some of the above categories to his passion. These are his comments on the categories that he felt needed improvement:

- **Addictiveness and flexibility** – most of the games I liked to play were good fun to begin with but after a short while I began to notice imbalances in them. By imbalances I mean little things that once you realised give you a massive advantage over your opponent. Little flaws in a game. A simple one would be *Connect4*. *Connect4* is very much like noughts and crosses only larger. Instead of three by three it is a seven by six column board and instead of noughts and crosses you use coloured counters which you slot into position. If you want to win you need to fill the middle column – if you know this you can win every single time. *Connect4* boils down to who can fill the middle column the fastest.

- **Playability** is the most important part of a game. Playability can be divided into a number of categories – the mechanics which everything is based on. Then a system that makes the game flow so that everyone enjoys it then finally you need a system that has been tested to extremes.

- **Design** – game boards should usually be interesting and eye grabbing when you take them out of the box. Mine isn't! Its very simple because the fun doesn't come from the board it comes from actually playing the game. If you get your fun from the board then the fun won't last long. My board is practically empty giving the players freedom to come up with new ideas and do their own thinking.

- **Shape** – the shape of my game pieces are designed to free flow around each other and can be easily moved between other pieces and be picked up easily. I was offered the chance to have my counters made flat in the factory like many other board games but for my game this would not work – mine needed to be tall.

- **Size** – the game is designed to be very portable, especially unusual for a strategy game. The size of the pieces and the hexagons on the board are very precise. A lot of other games don't have that level of thought or detail put into them.

- **Price** – my game is designed to be manufactured much more cheaply than other strategy games, including the most well known. The original game was very complex and would have been extremely expensive so I stripped it down, ensuring that I didn't cut down on the game's playability.

See the power of those categories when you apply them to your own product or service. We shall come across Robin again when we look at how to protect your ideas.

Exercise

Take your kettle, or a piece of furniture or even your car and apply negative thinking to it for ten minutes and see what happens. It can be a lot of fun and very stimulating. One young woman who applied this to her car decided that each engine part should be a different colour. She felt that this would make instruction manuals much easier to understand and also meant that she would be willing to carry out minor repairs herself. For example the car battery could be yellow while the starter motor is green with red spots. She felt this would make it easier for her to understand what mechanics were talking about – she obviously doesn't use the same garage as me! If you want, you can apply negative thinking to something that annoys you (you'll have already done this possibly without realising it).

In the next chapter we're going to look at a technique that I consider to be one of the most powerful in this book alongside that of the Ideas Matrix. Ideas Mapping is going to knock your socks off and turn you into a creative thinking superstar!

BRILLIANT BUSINESS IDEAS

EIGHT

IDEAS MAPPING

MOST PEOPLE HAVE HEARD ABOUT Tony Buzan and his mind mapping techniques. These techniques are great for revision, learning something new or planning something. I took the basic concept and created Ideas Mapping. This technique works on the observation that many companies operate back to front. They design a product/service then look for a market in which it can be sold. Ideas Mapping lets you pick a market and then design a product/service for that market. It's a very powerful technique that has produced some astounding results and it's also great fun. It's great for developing products for niche markets. It usually takes at least two people (if you really had to you could do it by yourself) and I would suggest no more than five be involved. There are some rules with this technique:

- Only one person uses the pen throughout the session.
- Once the pen has touched the paper it doesn't leave it until the ideas generation session has ended.
- Once the pen touches the paper it cannot stop moving – even if the questioner is hesitant or

stops for a while the pen must carry on moving even if it's just to draw a scribbled ball.

- The person with the pen must answer the questions out loud as he or she also answers them on paper.

- Only one person can ask the pen holder questions at any one time.

- The person asking the question must continue to ask the question until he or she is happy that they've got an intelligent answer.

- These sessions should be highly focused and without interruption. To get really good results both the person holding the pen and the questioner need to practice. For the person providing the answers it is almost a form of hypnosis, being completely focused on the page and the answers.

You need to sit around a table and have a blank sheet of A3 size paper. The person who holds the pen – who we shall refer to as the Scribe – should be the one who wants a business idea. The Scribe should decide on a market or customer profile upon which to concentrate. The profile should be relatively specific and should give at least the gender and age group of the target. Once that is established a symbol or word, which represents the target, is drawn in the centre of the sheet of paper. The session then begins and involves what I call: "the art of asking the right question at the right time". Those not holding the pen begin to ask questions about the target market. The Scribe must answer the questions verbally *and* in written form – be that words, symbols or rough drawings. The questioners might not understand what is being written/drawn on the paper but the Scribe will, which is all that matters.

The questioners should start off by asking about the typical passions of a target, their hobbies, those things that annoy or frustrate them and what they consider necessary to their survival (Ideas Matrix). Once they are satisfied with their answers (and sometimes these are the only questions that need to be asked) they can move onto the awkward questions and look at services/products/businesses already catering for the target market and so on. At the end of an Ideas Mapping Session the Scribe should be worn out and the paper should be covered in scribbles and doodles. If the session has been conducted properly then you'll definitely have some good ideas that you can research more thoroughly later on.

It is advisable when conducting an Ideas Mapping Session to either film it or record it.

Case Study

Amy was a student who wanted to set-up a part-time business as she realised that she would learn more than she would if she worked part-time in a bar or as a waitress. She came to me with an idea but after we researched it we saw that it was not viable. After a chat we decided to use Ideas Mapping to see what she could come up with. Below is our dialogue, which I have included in this way because it is important to see how I asked the questions and how we arrived at the end result.

J: OK so who are you going to choose for your target market?

Amy: Well I think I'll stick with the one I was targeting with the original idea.

J: And that was?

Amy: That was women of my age on campus *(eighteen to twenty-one year-olds)*.

J: Which is good because you should have a thorough knowledge of that market.

Amy: Exactly.

J: OK, well then in the middle of the paper I want you to draw a picture or write a word that to you symbolises your target market. It doesn't have to mean anything to me as long as you understand it. OK?

Amy: Yep (*she draws a stick figure wearing a dress*).

J: OK, Amy. Tell me, what is the customer passionate about? (*with this technique the more you know about your target market the better. If you know very little about it then it would be worth getting a representative in and doing an Ideas Matrix and an Ideas Mapping Session with them to get a good understanding of your future customers. Any market research will help – we will look at this more closely in the Ideas Checker chapter*).

Amy: Shopping, wine, socialising.

J: Start drawing and writing it on the paper. (*Amy draws lines away from the symbol and starts writing and drawing little pictures. For the shopping she draws a hand bag, for the drinking a bottle of wine for the socialising a small group of stick people*).

J: What hobbies does the target customer tend to have?

Amy: Keeping fit, reading chick-lit, watching films (*she draws more lines and starts drawing dumb-bells, a book and something I can't describe – remember, only she has to understand what she is putting on the paper. As long as I understand what she is verbalising*).

J: What really gets the target customer wound up and angry?

Amy: *Laughs.* Jerk boyfriends, bitchy girl friends, rude people, selfish people (*she writes words rather than drawings for this section*).

J: What does she consider necessary to her survival?

(*Amy starts drawing*).

J: What's that?

Amy: Err, it's a...a mobile phone... (*by now Amy is getting so involved in the Ideas Mapping session that she is forgetting to talk to me but is still answering my questions on the paper. This is good – as long as she answers me verbally when I prompt her – as it shows she is extremely focused on what she is doing. Some may compare this to an hypnotic trance and for the best results, this is what we want*).

J: Mobile phones. (*Laughs*) OK, what else? Food, survival, air, shelter, love? (*I often have to remind people of these because they often take them for granted but it is vital that they are included*).

Amy: Yeah...yeah all of them. (*She starts drawing a rough house, a heart and some other stuff*).

J: What else? (*she hasn't finished drawing but it is important that the session goes fast otherwise momentum will be lost. You need to slightly rush the Scribe to keep them focused*).

Amy: I don't want to sound shallow but looking good is important... (*my ears pricked up at this*)

J: Why is this important?

Amy: Well if you look good then you feel good and it's important to feel good

J: Why? Why is it important to feel good? (A*my has stopped drawing but the pen is on the paper and she is doodling in a corner – this is fine as long as she is thinking of an answer to my question*).
Amy: It is because most women like to feel and look good and society places that responsibility on us. It's not just about attracting men. (*She's starting to sound slightly defensive here*

so I need to change tack and use a different line of questioning).

J: I find that really interesting. What things does the target customer do to make herself feel and look good?

Amy: (*She starts drawing again*). Well; buying new clothes, going for a spa day and getting a facial, wearing and buying make up, going out with the girls.

J: Why do women wear makeup?

Amy: I just told you – to make themselves feel better!

J: Is there anything else connected to make up that women do?

Amy: Well...there's manicures... (*her eyes light up as an idea pops into her head*)

J: Can you do manicures?

Amy: Yes – In fact I'm very good at them. I could do them between lectures. I could do really good manicures within fifteen minutes...

The session was ended. Amy had found her idea. In the end she didn't go ahead with it for a variety of reasons but in my opinion it was a viable idea. Again the interesting thing is that Amy already had the skills she just hadn't made the connection. You will find that this is often the case and Ideas Mapping is a great way to help you realise it.

This is Amy's Ideas Mapping session. See how messy and disorganised it looks? Some of it you can't even read! It looks like someone has spent a few hours just doodling and scribbling! An interesting thing is that there is a lot of evidence that highly creative people often doodle and scribble when thinking. If you look at the papers of Leonardo Da Vinci – who I think you will agree could be considered highly creative – you will see that they are untidy and full of little drawings.

Another Case Study

Sam is a secondary school teacher who specialises in English Literature and Language. While he enjoyed his job he was also looking for a change and a little extra income. He came to see me and we decided that we would do an ideas mapping session together.

J: OK, Sam, so what market are you going for?

Sam: I'm going to go for the market I know best – teenagers at school.

J: I see so you're going for teenagers but in a specific context – school.

Sam: (*pause as he considers*) Yep.

J: Good stuff. You know the rules. Start drawing in the centre something that represents, to you, teenagers at school.

(*Sam draws a stick figure in a blazer holding a mobile phone*).

J: What are their passions? (*Sam starts drawing*). Remember; when I ask a question you need to answer out loud!

Sam: Their passions are their friends, socialising, football, netball, cars, music... (*he's too general so I need to make him go into more detail – I decide to do this by changing the question*).

J: What gets them angry and frustrated?

Sam: *Laughs*. Having to wear a school uniform, bad marks in their homework, most of them are really good people so such things as bullying... (*He draws a cloud with lightning strikes coming out of it above the stick figures head. He's still being slightly too general for my liking, which means that I have not yet asked the right question*).

J: OK, I now know what gets them frustrated and angry but what stresses them out? You know what I mean? What worries them?

Sam: The one big thing is exams! (*He writes the word exams in big capital letters in one corner of the page*).

J: Tell me more!

Sam: Well around GCSE time most of them start to get stressed. In fact I think they get too stressed. I don't want to play down the importance of the exams but it worries me when I see how stressed-out some of the pupils get. (*This is really interesting*

– not only is Sam telling me that a majority of the students get stressed-out by exams but that it concerns him that they do so. He has an emotional stake in this issue, whether he realises it or not, that suggests it may be worth looking at closer).

J: Why do they get worried about it?

Sam: Because, for those of them that care – and I have to say most of them do – they feel there's a lot riding on the grades they get. At that age when someone tells you it's important you tend to listen to them whether you let on or not. They each have a load of subjects to revise for, which can be stressful and then the actual exam conditions themselves are never really pleasant. Also – well I don't want to get into it in detail because it is slightly controversial –for many people exams are not an effective way of measuring their learning anyway – if you're like this it can really stress you out. Hell! To be honest, just the thought of exams can stress you.

J: Right. Do you think they would like to lessen the stress then?

Sam: *laughs*. Yeah – by not having to do exams!

J: Well we both know that won't happen. Remember you have to keep your pen moving at all times on the page. From what you're saying its the revision and the actual exam conditions that stress them out the most – is that right?

Sam: Well…yes. I mean no student really enjoys revision. Then, having to sit there in silence in a hall with a hundred other people and write can be quite intimidating. (*He scribbles something unidentifiable to me as he talks*).

J: So, what we're looking at is something that is going to help them with their revision and something that will ease the stress of exams when they are actually in that hall.

Sam: Yes, I think so.

J: So, how do pupils of that age usually revise? How can it be made more efficient and less stressful?

Sam: It's mostly from books, the notes they get given in class and, for many of them, whatever they can find on the internet. (*He draws books, a computer monitor and pieces of paper*).

J: Is this the best way to learn – in your opinion?

Sam: Not for everyone, no. (*Hesitates.*) I think the best way to learn is to use all your senses.

J: Tell me more – and remember; keep the pen moving!

Sam: Well, we encourage them to use mind maps and lots of colour. I also encourage them to have music on at a low level in the background. Although some of the parents are less than impressed with this (*laughs*). I think it helps them.

J: So you're using your eyes and your ears and you're missing out how many other senses?

Sam: Err...three. Touch taste and smell. (*At this point although I hate to admit it I was slightly lost – I wanted to move onto a different line of questioning as I felt I had taken Sam down a wrong path*).

Sam: Scratch-cards!

J: I'm sorry?

Sam: Scratch-cards. Cards that could help with revision. (*Although I have stopped, puzzled and slightly bewildered, Sam is drawing enthusiastically on the paper*).

Sam: Listen. Scratch-cards with scents in them. You know! Like they use in the Lottery except these have specific scents on them.

J: Explain to me how it would work – and keep on drawing!

Sam: I know for a fact that smell is a very powerful sense. In fact when I think about it I'm sure I read something about them using it to help old people with memory problems. They would make them smell something from their childhood and it would bring back a host of memories. Why can't we do the same with young people? Get them to revise and while they are revising make them use a scratch card with a particular scent. They then take another scratch card into the exam hall with them. They scratch it, sniff the scent and their memory is activated. Scents could also be used that calm people down. So it would help them deal with their stress levels in exams!

J: OK, so you've got a possible product there. We need to do more research but it's a start.

Sam: It certainly is.

We carried on the session for another fifteen-minutes and did another a few days later but this first idea was the one Sam liked the most. He is currently researching his idea to see if its viable and he kindly agreed to let me include this account.

The Importance of Questions and the Questioner

While the questions are based mostly around the other technique we have already covered, it's worth having a closer look at them as the importance of the questioner and the questions cannot be over-emphasised in this technique.

You will want to ask the following questions – it is up to you to decide what areas on which to specifically focus and question further.

- **What is your chosen market?**
  This may sound obvious but you need to ensure they have a very specific market in mind. It can't just be men or women; it has to be a particular group of men or and women. If they have difficulties with this then ask them what they believe the average age of their market is, the sorts of places they would live and so on. Pin them down on the market – this does pre-suppose some knowledge of the market. For this technique to be really effective this knowledge is needed.

- **What are their common hobbies?**
- **What are their passions?**
- **What do they regard as necessary to their survival?** Don't forget to add the crucial five – shelter, air, water, love, food.
- **Why do they see these things as necessary?**
- **Would they be willing to pay for that?**
- **What really frustrates them or makes them angry?**
- **How could you improve upon that?**
- **Where does the market commonly congregate?**
- **Can you find them on the internet easily?**
- **Are there any websites that they commonly use?**
- **Do they have a lot of available money?**

A good way to interrogate a person is to keep asking the question: Why? Why does the target market do that? Why do they do that? And so on.

One Final Tip

One entrepreneur who uses Ideas Mapping a lot had this to say:

"It may sound silly but I find it easier to make Ideas Mapping work for me if I give my market a name. So for example if my market was male students aged eighteen to twenty-one, I would call the symbol in the centre Tom. Personalising it made it easier for me to access the needs and wants of the market. I guess it works on the basis of that digital TV channel *Dave* – it was called that because everyone knows a bloke called Dave so the question was asked: What does Dave like to watch on the TV?

Exercise

Grab a friend and do a quick ten-minute Ideas Mapping session. Within ten-minutes you will see the power of this technique. If you don't have a partner, take a look at your Ideas Matrix and do a quick Ideas Mapping session based on it.

NINE

SOME GENERAL RULES FOR IDEAS GENERATION

HERE ARE SOME GENERAL RULES for Ideas Generation. Apply them to all of your creative thinking sessions and see the results.

- Let your mind go into free-fall and free-associate – let your mind make its own connections without your interference and see what happens. Whether you realise it or not your subconscious mind never stops working and making connections. This is why you dream. Most people have had the experience of sitting there, doing nothing, when suddenly the answer to a question they posed the day before pops in to their head. It's as though their mind was a computer and they sent it a request and then had to wait for the answer. It's the same with ideas. Find somewhere quiet and free from distraction and let your mind drift and see where it leads you.

- Do not judge or dismiss any idea your mind comes up with straight away – often you are not the best person to decide on the quality of your ideas! I often wonder how many brilliant ideas never become much more than a thought in someone's head because they dismiss the idea as unworkable the minute it pops in there. Also once you do have your idea be careful who you tell – do your own checking first before you share it with anyone. Nothing kills an idea faster than the scorn of another.

- Note down any ideas that you have as soon as possible – this is one rule that I confess I need to follow more often – I have a dozen good ideas a day (I've trained my brain to do this) but forget a fair few because I do not note them all down. I have a small notepad which I keep with me at all times. In fact I believe the very act of noting them down encourages my mind to come up with more!

- If an idea excites you then it is worthy of further development and examination – don't let other peoples judgement of your idea kill your excitement. Don't get hopeful and don't get despondent – put it through the checker, do some research and find out the reality. It's important not to let emotions cloud the issue – the time to get excited is after you've confirmed your idea is viable.

SOME GENERAL RULES FOR IDEAS GENERATION

- Whenever you are frustrated or angry there is an opportunity for Ideas Generation. As I said before you often get angry or frustrated because the strategy you're currently using isn't working for you – step back – recognise it as a chance to get creative and see what happens. Put that anger/frustration to good use.

- Having more than one person involved in the Ideas Generation process can help immensely! Just make sure when you are in a group that everyone is in agreement about how any ideas will be treated.

- Always put your ideas through the Idea Checker – this is really important – many people are initially reluctant to do this as they are afraid that their idea will not pass it but it's worth finding out earlier rather than later after you've put a lot of work into it. Remember that you will always have another idea – the human mind is incredible; if one idea doesn't work you can trust yourself to come up with another that will work.

- Generating ideas should be fun! If you do not enjoy using these techniques then your mind is not going to come up with much. The best attitude to adopt when using these techniques is playfulness. Do not put yourself under pressure and don't have high expectations –

just enjoy trying the techniques out and see what happens. The best time to be creative is when you have the time! Not when you actually need to be. Being creative under pressure is not always easy – condition your mind to be creative before the pressure is on.

- Maintain a sense of excitement and curiosity. This is tied into ensuring that you use these techniques with an attitude of playfulness and without high expectations. There is a universe of connections and wonderful ideas out there waiting to be discovered by you. Open your eyes and start asking questions. This requires some effort on your part but it's worth it.

- Give yourself an ideas quota – be it a certain number of ideas a month, a week or a day. Remember they don't have to be good ideas – just ideas. Once you've conditioned your brain to be more creative the ideas will flow. I give myself a quota of ten ideas a day. That's seventy ideas in a week, from which two or three are likely to be worth pursuing further.

Now that you know all of the techniques we are going to move onto the second stage of the Ideas Generation process. We're going to look at the Ideas Checker stage.

TEN

IDEAS CHECKER

I'M GOING TO ASSUME THAT you've not skipped any of the chapters up to now, that you've gone through the exercises and that you've come up with some ideas – some of which have excited you and which you want to explore in more detail. I know I've said this before – I'm going to say it again – this stage is crucial if you want to ensure that the ideas you have generated are viable, likely to be successful in the real world and you want to save yourself a lot of heartache – and possibly loss of money and energy.

Although this is the chapter that you are most likely to skip over or not spend too much time on, my recommendation is that, if you have an idea, you spend as long as you can on this stage.

Having said that, remember; the best test is reality! The most successful business ideas tend to have the following characteristics:

- They give significant value to the customer/end user.
- They solve a problem or answer a need, which someone is willing to pay for.
- They have a sizable market and a good profit potential.

- They are a good fit with your skills/talents likes and dislikes.
- There is a dependable source/supply chain.
- They have the potential for repeat purchases.
- They can be easily marketed or make good PR.
- There are no massive legal issues or regulations.

Based on the above we're going to look at a number of different areas and issues you need to consider when researching your idea. These areas and issues are:

- **Personal** – In this area we will ensure that not only is the idea right for you but that you are the right person for the idea. Just because you had the idea that doesn't mean you are automatically the best person to take it forward. If you're not, don't worry, this doesn't mean you can't benefit from your idea.

- **Market** – In this area we will ensure that your idea is fulfilling a need or a gap in the market. It's incredible how many people neglect this area basing their decisions on emotions or simply presuming that because they like the product everyone else will as well.

- **Financial** – in this area we will investigate whether the business is financially viable. To a large extent this can be a personal decision as it rests largely on your level of tolerance of risk.

- **Supply Chain** – We will check as to whether or not you have a supply chain and understand it.

- **Marketing** – Having a great idea that is right for you means nothing if it's impossible to communicate that idea to your target market. Very often the person who creates the product or who has the idea is not the right person to market it.

- **Resources** – Do you have all the resources or at the very least potential access to the resources that you need to make your idea a reality? In a perfect fair world your amazing, earth-shattering idea, would automatically get all the support it needs but we all know that things are rarely that simple.

- **Protection** – Can you protect your idea in anyway? How easy is it to copy? This can impact significantly on the viability and value of a product. It's a complex topic which is why protection will be looked at in the next chapter.

The checking stage involves a series of questions and some research on your part. I would encourage you to be completely honest when doing all of this.

Personal

We're going to start with personal because this book is about coming up with a business idea that is special to you. As I said in the introduction, if you personally buy into this idea – if it excites and interests you – then you are more likely to keep on going when things get tough. We're going to look at the personal aspects from a number of different areas.

Ethics, Values and Morals

First of all does this idea fit in with your own personal ethics and morals? For some people, getting involved in internet pornography holds no problems whatsoever – to them it is purely a lucrative business in which to get involved. Others wouldn't touch it. Do you have an interest in the environment that may conflict with the idea in some way? I would advise you to sit down and really think about this as often these types of conflicts only become visible once you are in the implementation stage. You really want to try and spot these conflicts and deal with them at the outset. If you plan to have partners in this business or have persuaded people to invest, then you may also want to pose this question to them. Again it would be wise to find out if they have any particular values or beliefs that may clash with your idea before anything is agreed.

Time

This is the one concern of everyone I have worked with to help develop their business ideas. Will I have enough time? Without wanting to sound pessimistic or scare you off, take the amount of time you think it will take you to set-up your business and double it. While I am of the opinion that if you really want something you will find the time for it you need to be honest with yourself – will you have the time to commit to this business? From another angle, is this the right time in your life for you to start developing a business? If you're in a relationship does your partner realise how much time it will take? Are they happy with it? Are they willing to support you? If you have children are they willing to bear most of the burden and realise that you may not be there all the time? Many people start their business while still in full-time jobs – if you are in this position then you need to be really sure you have planned your time out correctly.

Are you the right person?

Be honest with yourself! You've enjoyed using the ideas generation techniques and you've come up with some great ideas. The thought of having your own business fills you with excitement and you could dream about it all day. Are you the right person to do it? Only you will know – and even then you might not know for sure until you've tried it but let's see if we can get an inkling now.

Do you have the skill-sets you need to set-up this business? For example I am fairly certain that I could do a good job at marketing my business. I know without a doubt that I could not handle the financial accounts. I have been on a number of accountancy courses and still cannot get to grips with numbers – I simply do not have it in me. Sit down and make a list of your strengths and weaknesses – to ensure that you are being totally honest get someone else to sit down and run through the list with you. It's very hard for us to be objective about ourselves.

If, having thought about it and decided that you're not the right person for this idea, then you can still gain something from it. Could you find someone who could take your idea forward? If so could you sell the idea to them? Or could you become a sleeping partner? I have met a number of people with some fantastic business ideas that could quite clearly work and even more clearly they weren't the people to do anything with them. One of the ideas was so good that I asked the guy if I could take the idea and do something with it. He declined and at the time there was very little I could do. He did nothing with the idea and I know that someone is now running an identical business and doing very nicely out of it.

Partners

A lot of people go into business with partners, husbands, wives and friends. There's absolutely nothing wrong with this – having a partner brings an extra dimension to business – a whole load of advantages and disadvantages. A business partnership is like a marriage – you both have to work at it. If you are doing this then you need to sit down and discuss your strengths weaknesses, what each other expects from the other, and what happens if it all goes wrong. It would be worth having a partnership agreement drawn up even if your business partner is also your life partner.

Market

This is critical – is there a market for your product? Remember the example of Flooz, the online company? We frequently see people on *Dragon's Den* who have apparently amazing ideas but have no prospective customers whatsoever. It makes great entertainment but I can't help thinking that with a little bit of research the person with the idea would have found this out. How do you find out if there is a market? Well there are a variety of ways. Market research can be carried out online, face to face, with a product, without a product. The more work you put into getting to know your potential market the better. Idea Mapping is a great technique but it depends on some knowledge of the market (which is why most people who use this technique usually target their peers). If you're working with this technique and you're uncomfortably aware that most of the session was based on assumption then you need to do some research.

Where is your market going?

The one big thing that a lot of people forget especially when it comes to technological businesses is that the market is not static – it's constantly moving! You need to go where the market is going not where it is currently otherwise, six months down the line, you may find your idea is old and dying. This is where knowledge of the market comes in – a quick dip into the market is not enough; you need to know it as intimately as possible. There are companies out there who identify market trends. Find out where your market is moving to; not just where it is. One good website is wwww.trendspotting.com.

Competitors

Who are your competitors? By this I don't just mean the businesses who are selling a product or service similar to your own, but also those products or services that people are buying instead of yours. Find out as much as you can about them and if possible actually experience their products or services for yourself. Get copies of their financial records if they have registered with Companies House – this will give you some idea of the size and profitability of the market you are planning to go into, as well as show you how well your competitors are doing. Make a list of their strengths and weaknesses – what do they do well and not so well. Apply the negative thinking technique to your competitors. Areas to consider are:

- Financial stability
- Marketing
- Popularity
- Product/Service quality
- Size of customer market
- Premises (if they have them)

Financial

Do you have the financial resources to start this business? Most business ideas take money to set-up and develop. You need to work out how much you will need and will probably need at least fifty per-cent more than you've initially calculated! In an ideal world you would also have an emergency fund to cover any unforeseen circumstances.

Do you have access to financial resources? If you don't have enough money can you get access to money? This could be from family, friends, potential investors, venture capitalists, business angels or (rare these days) a bank. If you do borrow money from friends or family, ensure – before you accept a penny –

that you have an agreement with which all parties are happy, which is printed and signed with each party getting a copy.

How long before your business will be self sustaining? To answer this question you need an in-depth knowledge of your market. You need to calculate how long it will be before your businesses income covers its costs. A lot of businesses make a loss in the first six to twelve months. It's a personal decision but you need to decide how long you can hold on before the business starts paying for itself. Be conservative when estimating the revenue. Be liberal when estimating the costs.

How long before your business will be profitable? How long will it be before the business not only covers its costs but makes extra money? Can you wait for this length of time? If you are involving investors will they realistically be willing to wait this length of time before they see the rewards for their investment? Again you need to be conservative but realistic when it comes to this.

Sustainability of idea. Businesses can very rarely survive on one product or one idea. If you have an idea for one product what can you do to make it sustainable? By this I mean at some point it is likely that people will stop buying it – can you modify it to make it sufficiently different? Do you have other product ideas that you can implement after the first one? Is your idea little more than a passing fashion or a fad? Or is it ideally a repeat purchase product that people will have to or want to keep on buying? I have had a large amount of people come to me with what they consider to be a business idea but which in actual fact is a product idea. There is a big difference.

Protection

How easy is it to copy your idea? Is your idea very complex? Does it require specific skill-sets that are rare? Is it easy to copy? If so how are you going to prevent others from copying it? Remember the Ideas Heist! If your idea is hard to protect then it is ripe for someone else to take and implement elsewhere or even worse in the same area! This happened with smoothie bars in our area where at one time we had seven bars – quite a few closed within a very short time.

Can you patent/copyright/trademark your idea? If you watch *Dragon's Den* then you will notice that one of the things they always ask is if the idea patented. You can see the rapid loss of interest by the Dragons if the answer is negative. If there is a market for your idea and you can patent it or trademark it then that idea is ultimately more valuable. Patenting can be a complex and costly business and it is wise to get professional advice. If you believe that your idea can be patented then your first stop should be the IPO website (Intellectual Property Office).

Can you protect your idea in any other way? If you can't patent your idea is there any other way you could protect it? One guy I worked with for some time, designed computer software. He would deliberately write errors into the software so that if someone copied it he would be able to prove it by highlighting the errors in the copied software.

Are you too late? If you have an idea that you believe is patentable then you would be wise to find out if someone has beaten you to it. You can do this online at http://www.ipo.gov.uk/types/patent/p-os.htm or you can use their Search and Advisory Service, which will carry out the research for you. They reckon on a ten-day turn-around. Both will involve a fee but you would be well advised to use one of them if patenting is your intention.

More information on protecting your idea with a focus on IPR (Intellectual Property Rights such as copyright and patents) is in the next chapter.

Marketing

How easy is it to communicate your idea to your target market? Is your idea/business highly complex? Can you communicate it to the target market easily?

This is a highly important question and again it's one that many of the people who go before the *Dragon's Den* seem to neglect. It's all very fine having a wonderful product/service but if the people it is aimed at can't understand it then they won't buy it.

What is the message that you want to communicate to potential customers? This relies on you having a thorough knowledge of your customers. What will they respond to? How can you stand out from your competition? A lot of marketing is common sense and there is a huge amount of information on the internet. The internet itself is a fantastic marketing medium depending on your business. Bottom line: you need to know what will get your customers coming to you.

Do you require a lot of resources to market your product/service? Every now and then someone comes to me with an idea that is fantastic and would no doubt work. The problem is that these ideas would require vast amounts of money and resources to actually market them and make them work. In an ideal world such a person would be able to find an investor or a partner but that doesn't always happen. If this is the situation you find yourself in and you can't find access to the resources needed then you need to ask yourself how else can you benefit from your idea?

Are there any traditional routes for marketing for your business? Some businesses are marketed in a particular way and the customer expect this so that they know where to look. For example most plumbers and electricians will advertise in the Yellow pages. Most web designers will advertise online. What are the traditional marketing mediums for your idea? Note that just because there may be traditional mediums for marketing does not mean you can be lazy about it. You should still be seeking other and more effective ways to market your product.

Supply Chain

Can you trust your suppliers? If you have any can you trust them? Are they dependable? At the very least you will want to get information on their financial status. The last thing you need is for your suppliers to go bankrupt when you have customers waiting. You can do this a variety of ways. You would do well to check out their reputation with other customers of theirs. Even if they have a good reputation, follow your instincts. Are they helpful and friendly with you? Can you see yourself working with them on a long-term basis? Do they take an interest in what you are doing?

Is your supply chain complex or simple? By supply chain we mean how the product goes from manufacture, through storage and distribution, to being presented to the customer. In terms of this book I have a very simple supply chain. I write the book and put it onto the internet. People log onto the website, enter their credit card details and then download the book. I have worked with people whose business ideas necessitate hugely complex supply chains which inevitably bring a whole new series of challenges. One example is two young men both of whom were named Andy. They came to me with an idea about tailor-made suits. They intended to have these suits made in China according to measurements taken in the UK and sent across by email. The suits would then be shipped to the UK. Despite warnings about the complexity and problems inherent in such a chain, they went ahead and experienced the following:

- **The cultural differences between China and the UK** – for example their order was delayed a number of weeks while China celebrated a national holiday.

- **The language problems** – they spoke no Chinese so brought in a Chinese interpreter to help them out. Unfortunately he did not always translate correspondence accurately, which created more problems.

- **Delivery problems** – shipping and delivery difficulties meant that another order was delayed and when the products finally arrived, some had been damaged in transit.

I don't want to scare you from having a complex supply chain. The two Andies could have avoided many of the problems had they taken the time to research Chinese business culture, got themselves a fully trained translator and planned their delivery routes a bit better. So, what I will say is that if you have a complicated supply chain, do your research properly. If any part of your chain makes you feel uncomfortable that means there's a potential problem with it.

Linked to all of this is geography. It might be wise to have a supplier in your own country. What if there are quality problems? What steps does your supplier have in place to remedy them and make sure that your business is not damaged? If they're geographically closer, it should be much easier to resolve problems when they occur.

Other Resources

Facilities and Premises. Does your idea require facilities and premises? Some of the ideas I have encountered require only a computer and connection to the internet. Others need a building in a particular location. If your idea is like this do you have access to the facilities/premises that you need or do you have the resources to locate and rent or buy them? If your idea is to run a tea-room in a city centre then the chances are you will need a business loan or backer – unless you have access to a large amount of money. I've known people who want to set-up their own night club or bar and yet confess that they have no money at all to invest into their idea.

What contacts and resources do you have to help with the implementation of this idea? Who do you know that can help you with this idea? It's amazing how many people have fantastic contacts that would be more than willing to help them but for some reason they don't seem to make the connection. I believe half the problem is that many people do not regard family and friends as contacts. All family and friends – be it your father, your sister, or your sisters best friend – are contacts and they are there to be utilised. So use them! Make a list of the people that you know, their areas of speciality, occupation, interests, contacts that they have. Any contacts they have are now your contacts! In terms of resources this includes your local library, chamber of commerce and any business support units or facilities in your area. If you have access to the internet then you have a wealth of resources – in fact your problem will be deciding which resource to call upon. See the back of this book for useful contacts and websites.

What other resources might you need to call upon? Besides the contacts and resources you already have, what other resources do you need – or think you might need – but have no access to at the moment? Make a list. It could include anything from premises to accountancy advice. You need to start exploring ways in which you could get these resources. As mentioned before, the internet is a good place to start – the government is eager to encourage people to start their own businesses and there are plenty of business support facilities out there that are often underutilised.

Legal. Are there any legal issues you need to consider? Any licenses or certificates that you need to run your business legitimately? For example if you're preparing and serving food then the very least you will need is a health and hygiene certificate and most probably approval from the local government. Research this area very carefully – it's much too important to leave to chance. One of the first places to contact would be your local council.

There's a lot of things to consider but hopefully as you are working your way through them you are finding that your idea is condensing and you are getting increasingly more excited about it. Bear in mind that a negative answer to these questions does not always mean that you need to ditch your idea – it may be that you merely need to tweak or mutate it – ideas rarely come out of the checker completely unchanged. To answer many of these questions you will need to rely on your common sense and instincts before deciding whether or not you want to continue.

ELEVEN

IMPLEMENTATION

YOU'VE GENERATED YOUR IDEA. You ran it through the Ideas Checker, did some research and found that it's potentially viable. It's time to make it a reality. We are more concerned with the generation of ideas in this book but I felt there had to be a chapter on implementation if only for the sake of completion. That said, the setting up a business is, of course, a creative act in itself.

We have already looked at implementation in the Ideas Checker but one of the big things to consider beforehand is the level of risk you are willing to take and how much you can mitigate it. For example if you can test your idea out on the market in a small way to begin with, then do so. Some ideas need to just be implemented and at times speed is of the essence if you want to beat the competition. If you've gone through the Ideas Checker then you will know by now which category you fall into.

Business Plan

I don't believe that a business plan is essential – one highly successful entrepreneur that I know has never written a business plan and wouldn't know how to – but I do believe they are important. Having a business plan helps because:

- You have something to show investors, banks and potential allies.
- You have something to measure yourself by.
- Like the Ideas Checker the simple act of writing out your intentions makes you think about it and discovering potential challenges.

If your business is relatively simple to set-up and you don't need any formal support then you may not need a business plan. If you are looking for a business loan or investors then you will almost certainly need a business plan. Again by now you should know whether you will or won't. At the very least, aside from the financial aspects of the business, you will need to be able to answer the following:

- **Who** – Who are your customers? Who are your allies/contacts? Who are your competitors?
- **What** – what is it that you are actually offering? What is it that your product or service offers to the customer? What problem does it solve? What value does it offer? Essentially why would someone pay for what you are offering?
- **Why** – Why are you doing it? Is it to make money? If so why do you need money? Is it to make the world a better place? Knowing why you are doing it (and there's no real right or

wrong answer) will help when the going gets tough (and it will) and keep you motivated so that you keep going.

- **When** – When do you plan to actually offer the service or product? Decide on a date when you will get your first customer and work backwards from there. What do you need to do before then to reach that point? By the time you have finished answering this question you should have a fairly detailed timeline.

- **How** – How do you plan to tie all of the above together? How are your allies and contacts going to help you?

If you can answer the above in detail and add the financial details (costs, potential profit, turnover, etc) then you are well on your way to implementing the idea.

If you do need a business plan there are countless books available on business planning and plenty of information and templates on the internet that you can pick up for free so we won't go through all the details of a business plan here. However, some of the things I believe are critical to the a good business plan are:

- **Executive Summary.** The summary is at the beginning of the business plan and it will be the first thing that a potential investor will read. If this does not grab the investor then chances are you have lost them. So what should be in your Executive Summary? I always say that you should think of it as if your business was a DVD and the Executive Summary was the blurb on the back and the front of the cover. It should provide the reader with the following information:

- A hook – this is something that will grab the readers interest straight away. Often it takes the form of a quote, a fact or a question.
- Basic information about the product or the service you are proposing to offer.
- Size of the market that you will be entering.
- Potential turnover and profit in the first three years.
- How much investment you require.
- Most of this information you will have gathered in the checker stage so it is merely a case of putting it all together and making it sound interesting.

- **Introduction.** An overview of the business, its origins and why you are setting it up. Also include here what the current status of the business is and where you are in terms of setting up.

- **Objectives.** Be sure to make your objectives as clear, concise and specific as possible (it often helps to use the SMART principle when formulating your objectives – (SMART stands for Specific, Measurable, Achievable, Realistic, Time-bound). Check that they fit in with your finances and plans elsewhere in the business plan – it's amazing how many people forget this. Most people divide them into short term, medium term, long term.

- **Competition.** If I received a pound every time someone told me that they had no competition, I would be very wealthy! Find out who your main competitors are and research them thoroughly. Do a SWOT (Strengths, Weaknesses, Opportunities, Threats) Analysis and compare them honestly to your business.

- **Operations.** How will you run your business? What are the logistics behind it? Are there any manufacturing processes involved in your business?

- **Risk Management.** What are the inherent risks in your business? Are there any health and safety issues? How do you plan to deal with them?

- **Finances.** Profit and Loss forecast, cash-flow forecast, investment needed and initial start-up costs.

- **Appendices.**
    - Financial projections for at least two years.
    - Any technical specifications, designs, blue prints.
    - Include a brief one-page CV of yourself and your partner(s).
    - Any additional information relevant to the business and likely to be of interest to the intended reader.

For more information on business plans including templates put the term "business plans" into an internet Search Engine.

Allies and Mentors

Time and again I've seen the usefulness of having mentors and allies. I'm not keen on the word "mentor" for various reasons but I don't have a better word and I'm not fond of "business coach" either. You want someone who is successful in business and would be willing to sit down with you and discuss the lessons they have learned and the mistakes they have made. A good mentor can really help you with the implementation of your plan and accelerate your businesses development. There are a number of organisations round the UK that provide access to mentors free of charge in an effort to encourage people to start their own businesses. If there is nobody suitable in your family or circle of friends that you could ask then access these services. The characteristics of a good mentor are:

- They are honest with you and admit when they don't know something.
- They will discuss *with* you rather than talk *at* you.
- They will have extra resources and contacts that can help you.
- They will not make decisions for you or force their own preferred actions on you but will discuss your options with you.

When you are beginning to implement your business ask yourself how much you can get for free. Do not be afraid to negotiate with people or be afraid to be "cheeky". When your business is just being born it needs as much help as it can get. If you're wondering what the best business structure is to form or whether or not you need an accountant and where can you find a good one then Business Link is a good place to go. The image of the lone entrepreneur making it on his own is more often than not a lie – you need a support group around you.

Action

Don't keep putting things off until the conditions are perfect. I have worked with a number of people who aren't willing to start their business until they have their glossy business cards and shiny brochures. Now obviously you need to present and maintain a professional image but at the same time *action* is the most important thing. Conditions are never going to be perfect and you can fret too much about image, values and so on. Make sure you're in a position to service a customer and then get out there and get them. A question you should ask yourself is how you can get what you want as fast and as easily as you can without compromising your idea and vision. Do you really need a property to start your business? Do you really need a super-duper website to kick things off?

Networking

I'm a big believer in networking. When in the process of setting up your business start attending as many networking events as you can. Join your local chamber of commerce – they usually run new members evenings where you will get a chance to introduce yourself and your business. A lot of people dislike networking either because they hate the thought of having to make conversation with strangers or because it sounds boring but if done right it can be very valuable. My tips would be:

- Always go to networking sessions with a plan or goal in mind – who do you want to see there? Why do you want to see them?

- Remember to take your business cards with you – the number of people who forget (including myself) is surprising.

- Always try to add value to the people you meet. For example if you meet a plumber and your friend was moaning about a leak in the house take his card and make sure you give it to your friend. Human beings are in general reciprocal creatures – if you help them, most of them will do their best to help you.

- When you are there remember why you're there – to get business or contacts who can help you get business. Look upon everyone you meet as being either a potential client/customer or someone who will spread the word about you.

- All too often at networking events people will get trapped in conversations that are going nowhere and are not business related and therefore a waste of their time. While obviously there has to be an exchange of pleasantries you are there to get contacts so don't be afraid to say to people: "It's very nice to meet you. Thank you for your card. I'd better get around and talk to more people." Say it in a pleasant manner and most people will not be offended.

- Follow up on any potentially useful contacts you meet as soon as you can. A simple telephone call or email should suffice.

Marketing

You should know your market extremely well by now having researched it at the checker stage. Marketing is a specialist topic and this is very general but you should be aiming to get more out than you put in. For example one company I know spends thousands on leaflets. To get a return on those flyers they only need four people to buy their products and past experience has taught them that they will get much more than this. One entrepreneur I work with uses what he calls bottomless marketing. He has managed to work out in his business how much on average each customer is worth to him over the average customer lifespan. This then gives him a marketing budget to play with. For this to work your marketing needs to be as targeted as possible – that is focused on a specific group or specific person. Your earlier work on identifying your target customer will be invaluable.

In the next chapter we look at protecting your idea. For those of you with an invention or specific product this is one of the things you will want to consider before setting up.

TWELVE

HOW TO PROTECT YOUR IDEA

YOU'VE GOT A FANTASTIC IDEA and of course you want to make sure that no-one else will steal it. In this chapter we are going to look at the various ways you can protect your idea in a little more detail. The information in this chapter is based on advice provided by the IPO. For more detailed information, go to http://www.ipo.gov.uk. In my experience the people who work in the Intellectual Property Office are extremely helpful and knowledgeable – if you have any questions then don't hesitate to contact them.

There are four main types of IPR (Intellectual Property Rights).

Design Rights

Design rights protect the actual design of an object – this includes the shape, size and visual appeal of an object. What it does not do is protect two-dimensional aspects such as patterns on the objects. For a design to be eligible for protection it must be new and unique, in which case both the external appearance and internal aspects can be protected. Like copyright, design rights are conferred automatically upon the designer. To strengthen the design rights protection you can register it, which prevents anyone from designing similar products independently and allows you to either sell or licence the design.

Copyright

Copyright can be applied to the following types of ideas:
- Literacy work – literature, poems, books, articles
- Dramatic work – scripts, plays
- Musical work – song lyrics and the actual music
- Recordings of work
- Broadcasts of work – radio/TV

Copyright gives the holder exclusive rights for a set amount of time. It is actually conferred upon the holder automatically but only protects the idea once it has been made real. So for example you must have written the book before you can claim copyright on the idea behind the book.

Trademarks

Trademarks can be used to protect your brands or signs that make your product or service stand out from those of your competitors. They can be used to protect words, names, symbols, sounds, colours, logos. You will need to renew the trademark every ten years and will be able to use the symbol ™ when you have it. You cannot trademark the following:

- A logo or symbol that is offensive or against the law or is seen as deceiving the public – for example, endowing your products or service with a quality they do not have.

- A symbol or logo that describes your goods or services or their characteristics: for example: "Open 24 Hours" could not be trademarked because it is a very common term in business.

- A symbol or logo that is common in your industry or business area.

- A symbol or logo that is not particularly distinctive.

Once you have trademarked something you have the right to put the symbol ® next to it. Trademarks give you protection from people using your logo or symbol and enables the law (usually Trading Standards) to prosecute anyone who copies your mark. You can, in the future, either sell or license your trademark. If you decide not to trademark then you still have protection in the eyes of the law. If someone uses your mark without asking for your permission then you can take them to court for the act of "passing off". To do this you would need to prove that the mark is yours and that they have damaged your reputation and business in some way.

Patents

Patents are probably one of the best known forms of IPR. Certainly if you watch *Dragon's Den* then you will notice it is the form of IPR they (the Dragons) ask about. Patents are used to protect new inventions, features and processes that make things work. They can protect for up to a maximum of twenty years. They give you legal rights in the event of someone making, using or selling the invention without your permission. To be eligible for patenting your invention must have the following features:

- It must be new! If someone has already created it then you will not be able to patent it.

- Have an inventive step. The easiest way to describe this would be to ask how imaginative was that? Was it a fairly obvious modification? Or did it take some skill and thought? If it's not obvious, it's probably inventive.

- Must be capable of being made or used in industry.

You cannot protect the following:

- Scientific (or mathematic) discovery or theory.
- Artistic/musical/dramatic work (i.e. copyright protected).
- A way of performing a mental act (i.e. way of doing businesses).
- A method of diagnosis or medical treatment.

The important thing to note about patents is that no-one must know about your invention before you have patented it. If they do then this could undermine or negate your application. This is something to bear in mind when doing ideas generation sessions in groups.

Remember! A UK patent will only protect your idea in the UK. A company overseas can copy your invention unless you patent it in that country as well! Patent laws vary from country to country so beware! If you are planning to patent in a multitude of countries then it may be worth looking into using the Patent Cooperation Treaty which you can apply for through the IPO. If you want to patent in only a few countries then it would probably be worth patenting them individually through their own offices. For more information on the worldwide patents go to http://www.ipo.gov.uk/types/patent/p-manage/p-abroad/p-worldwide.htm. If you plan to patent in Europe then look at the European Patent Convention http://www.ipo.gov.uk/types/patent/p-manage/p-abroad/p-europe.htm

Trade Secrets

If you have something that you want to keep a secret but it's not suitable for IP then trade secrets may be the way to go. If it's something that is difficult to replicate and you can establish that the information is confidential then you can draw up and have people sign a Confidentiality Agreement before you disclose your idea to them. This gives you recourse to legal action if they disclose the information you have shared with them. This will not, however, protect you if someone else independently comes up with the same idea. For a sample Confidentiality Disclosure Agreement go to http://www.ipo.gov.uk/types/patent/p-about/p-need/p-need-secret.htm

Case Study: Robin and Total Strategy

He decided to get it licensed so that he could sell it in the shops and realised that he would have to protect it. He first looked at patents but soon realised that you cannot patent a board game. A board game is not just a board game it is a collection of elements. For example:

- Dice rolling – can't patent it as it is in many games.
- Counter moving – many games have this.
- Cards to denote what is going on – many games have this.
- A board that folds – many games have this.

The above are the four most common things in a board game and you cannot patent them because it would infringe massively upon the games industry. All you can do with a board game is copyright it and trademark it.

Robin: To copyright it, I put the famous © symbol on it before printing. This means it is automatically copyrighted. This is a good deterrent but anybody with half a brain will want to protect further if they can because it is not copy proof. If it went to court I would have to prove the copyright and if someone challenged it this could be difficult. The most basic way to prove copyright is to send the document or item by registered post to yourself and don't open it – keep it in a drawer somewhere safe. Again this is a safeguard but in court it might be overruled. This means that you will want a second level. I took a picture of the game, a copy of the rules, photographs of the pieces and copies of the original art work. Having collected all that together, the plan was to give it to a separate organisation for safe keeping – for example a bank or a lawyer. I gave mine to a bank. It is date stamped so that each time I access it my visit is recorded. The trick is to never access it unless it comes to court in which case you give permission for the court to open it and it will be dated. A challenger would then have to prove that he or she had the idea before that date. For me this was ample copyright. I pay a monthly fee with the bank but it's a tiny amount and well worth it from my point of view. This was enough for me to then show it to board game companies. In the beginning I also asked them to enter Non Disclosure Agreements (NDA). If they didn't, my copyright precautions gave me sufficient confidence to send the game to them on-trust anyway.

I soon discovered that asking for NDAs makes a really bad first impression. I found that a lot of people found NDAs obnoxious, feeling that their integrity as individuals was being brought into question unnecessarily. So I quickly realised that a request for an NDA will often make a company take a step back. There may be a fear that they may hear an idea similar to one they have already thought of (this is a reason why many companies will not accept submissions from outsiders) which can lead to a whole host of problems. If you think about it, I was approaching companies and asking them nicely to take a look at my game and then dropping an NDA on them which basically says I don't trust them, yet I was asking them to risk an investment in me and my game. A better system of protection is to judge the character of the games company by researching them before making an approach. Decent, reputable companies thrive off new ideas and will take a good game to market professionally and with great integrity.

An additional element to my protection was that the game I presented was one of a series. Companies only saw one part of it which meant that if they liked the game and saw its potential, they would want to work with me on the whole series.

My approaches were unsuccessful to begin with – it was during a recession and my product cost too much to manufacture *en masse*. I stripped it down, making it as cheap as possible to manufacture without it losing its potential for complexity if wanted. I submitted the stripped down version to companies and made some great contacts and friends within the industry along the way. In fact for every company I approached I would get on average one referral to another company! The recession, however, rapidly killed off many of the small and medium sized game businesses that I approached. I tried Europe and the USA but had no luck there either. I felt that I had tried the best companies – the ones I really wanted to work with. The time I spent doing this was invaluable and I now have a set of contacts that I trust implicitly and in whom I can confide and run new ideas past.

    I heard that mobile phone games were squashing the board game market so I approached Microsoft. They had a new device which was essentially a table top touch screen technology. They weren't really interested in what I was doing but I liked the idea of touch screen and knew that Apple did a similar thing. I realised that I knew someone who developed games and apps for the iPhone. My contact proved to be interested and started making the iPhone game based on the board game that I designed.

    I decided to go into business for myself and realised that I needed two things – a trademark and a company to own the trademark. I also realised that branding was vital to the potential success of my business so the company is called *Total Strategy* – same as the game. I also thought that this would allow me to avoid trademarking. I thought that it would be difficult to steal the board game name when the company of the same name owned it. I was wrong! I had to trademark and I decided to do this in the USA because the biggest market for iPod games is there and Apple and the iStore are also based there. If someone steals something from the iStore, wherever they are in the world, they are stealing from the USA! A USA trademark gives me the most inexpensive international trademark protection I can get without going down the expensive world-wide protection route.

I bought two categories of trademark protection – one for board games and one for software games – which cost me roughly $500. This protected the software as well as is possible. I could get a world-wide trademark but I don't believe it is cost effective for me. Go for the biggest market! For me, that was the States. A trademark lasts for six months unless you can prove that you are trading in which case it lasts for years. It's still pending for me.

To get it I took my logo I went on the US government web page for its IPR office.

My application was in three stages:

First stage was submitting the logo with my name and address. In the USA you would normally have to pay the fee for trademarking ($500) and the legal fees, which can sometimes be more than the cost of trade-marking itself. Luckily I had a friend who knew how to do it so all I had to pay was the money for the trademark.

Second part of the application was the submission and approval stage. This is where your application is looked at by a lawyer in the USA to make sure that your forms have been completed correctly and that the legal description is right – you can't just enter: *a silver dragon logo on a black background*. It needs to be written in tight, legal language. When it's approved by the lawyer (he sent me a few tweaks) you then go through to publishing and rejection. This is where your application is published in a journal and anyone can challenge it if they so wish.

If no-one challenges it, your application goes through to the final stage which is the granting of the application. This is when you get your certificate to say that you hold the trademark. After I did this I then applied for a UK trademark which cost me £250. I did this because the board game is sold in the UK not in the USA. I applied for a trademark in the board game category. This is where I currently stand – I am now as protected as I can be. All I can do now is get the game out there and get some sales. In my view that is the ultimate protection – be the first and be as fast as possible.

Case Study: Rick

Rick knew from bitter experience that it was vital to protect his ideas and products as much as possible.

Rick: When I was younger I was maybe too trusting. I did some work for this guy and he went ahead and made a load of money from my designs and there was nothing I could do about it. When I came up with my ideas for cardboard furniture I was determined to protect them. I was in a cafe and I quickly sketched my idea on a napkin. I then went to a local company my brother worked at and asked them if they had any surplus material they wouldn't mind giving me. They kindly gave me a load and I took it home and made a full size mock up of a seat. I sat on it and got members of my family to sit on it and I made sure that it worked. The feedback from them was that it was great to sit on and it could take their weight easily.

I contacted Business Link and explained to them what I had done and asked for advice on how to protect my prototype. They sent me a confidentiality agreement which I took back to the company who had given me the materials and asked if they would work with me. I approached them because to my mind they had the infrastructure to mass-manufacture my seats whereas I had no way of doing it. They signed the agreement and I worked with their development department. They gave me costings for the product.

By this time I was unemployed so I went to Business Link and asked for more help. They offered me the services of a patent agent. He gave me free advice and looked at my designs. He carried out a patent search to ensure that there was nothing out there similar to my designs. I had two designs at the time and it turned out that one of them was totally unique and fully patentable and one was similar to other designs in another country, so I couldn't patent it but I could get it design registered. The issue of cost raised its head – protecting designs is very expensive. I managed to get the money and moved onto the next stage.

To get them protected I needed to get the patent agent to write a report for me. Once the report was compiled (it consisted of descriptive and technical data) it was put forward for acceptance. It took two years for the entire process – the report was submitted in 2002 and I got a letter confirming success of the application in 2004. During that two year wait I was able to put "patent pending" on my products which protected them to some extent and while I had that protection I got into as many local and regional papers as I could and ensured that I kept the press cuttings and magazine articles. My patent lawyer had told me to build up a history of usage. This means that if anyone had decided to contest my designs then I could prove when I had established them. It was a great feeling to finally get that letter telling me I had been successful.

The process is complex and you need to put your trust in the patent lawyer – taking part in the process really opened my eyes to how much work goes into these things. I really believe that you need a patent lawyer to guide you such a complex specialist area and, while its fascinating, I certainly wouldn't feel confident to go into it on my own.

A major consideration is the amount of money needed. As I've already said, it is very expensive and there are also renewal fees for both forms of IPR that I have.

You also need to be strategic about the forms of IPR you go for – you really need to think about which forms are best for you and make sure you get expert advice.

Once you can put "patent pending" on your product get as much evidence as you can that the design is yours – pictures, articles and times and dates.

Maybe it's because I've been stung before but I am still wary – even with the patents. I contacted a major global company and told them about my products and that I had a patent on one of them and the other had a registered design. I asked them to sign a confidentiality agreement but they refused, telling me that they were probably working on something similar, which I thought was utter rubbish and decided not to bother with them anymore. If they had ripped-off my designs, even though I had protection I wasn't certain that I had the resources to fight them in court. I really felt at their mercy. You've got to be careful even after you have the patent – not paranoid just careful. Apart from protection the other thing that really helps is speed to market. That's really important. If I'd known then what I know now I would have got my products out into the market five to six years earlier than I actually did. The trick is to get in there first and then move on to the next things while your competitors are just catching you up. Unfortunately, for a number of reasons, it didn't quite happen this way for me but I'm getting there now.

You have just read two peoples experiences with IP. They are talking about IP in specific contexts – most specialists would recommend the following:

1. Check you aren't infringing on another's IP! – In your excitement at having come up with a new idea you may well infringe upon someone else's intellectual property rights. To check if you have infringed, contact the Intellectual Property Office.

2. Use NDAs – People can be excessively paranoid about telling others their ideas. Obviously you wouldn't want to tell a potential or definite competitor about your wonderful new invention but the truth is that most humans don't have it in them to copy another person's idea. Most people will think "good idea!" but they won't be prepared to put the work in and copy it. Nevertheless, to be cautious it would be wise to get anyone with whom you are discussing your idea on a more than casual basis, to sign a Non Disclosure Agreement. This will help ensure that the signer keeps your idea a secret and gives you legal recourse if they do not.

3. Use ™ with your logo in the UK – Putting ™ on your logo in the UK will discourage those people who might otherwise copy it. You may as well use this as it is free.

4. Identify your copyright © and date it – copyright is automatically conferred upon the person who created the work. Record the date on which you created it and, just to be sure, send a copy to yourself by registered post and keep it safe and unopened.

5. Protect your designs (date them) – same as above

6. Patent pending – file when you know you want to Patent.

7. If you aren't sure, ask for advice (although it may cost you). Patent solicitors are often expensive but some of them will give basic advice for free.

8. Have an IP strategy! – The IPR of your idea can be very valuable and make your idea extremely attractive to potential buyers/investors. If you intend to use IPR think very carefully about the best type and the best way to go about it. Robert's account is a good example of someone thinking very strategically about his IP.

THIRTEEN

HOW TO SELL YOUR IDEA

YOU'VE TRIED OUT THE TECHNIQUES outlined in this book and come up with a few ideas. You ran them through the Ideas Checker and one of them checked out. You have an idea that at the very least is viable, but for some reason you don't want to set-up or produce the idea yourself. It may be that while the idea is valid you don't have the resources and are unlikely to have them in the near future. It may be that you've decided having your own business is not for you but you still want to benefit from your idea. The answer then is to sell it.

Selling an idea is a huge topic and so this chapter necessarily has to be general.

Most companies will not even consider buying an idea unless you have the following:

- Protection
- Proof that the idea works

Protection

Companies, especially the larger ones, spend massive amounts of money on research and development, employing entire departments of people to come up with ideas. If you approach them either in person or electronically and tell them you have an idea the chances are they will refuse to see or listen to you or may not even read your email. They may well be developing something similar to your idea and if you've told them about your idea or sent information to them through the post or by email then you've put them in a difficult place. Imagine if you took an idea to a company and they rebuffed you then six months later bring something out that's very much like your product. Chances are a legal situation would result which would be costly and stressful for everyone concerned and a lot of bad press. To counter this, to look professional and to protect both you and the company you need to protect your idea as much as possible – the ultimate being a patent.

Proof that the idea works

Very few companies will be prepared to simply buy an idea – even if they do you will not get much for it. They will want to see proof that it works and that there's a market for it. This means you will have to have a prototype made. There are a number of companies that will be willing to make a prototype for you – have a look on the internet. This means that you will be spending money but if you're confident in your idea then you can consider it an investment. If your idea is a service then the chances are that a company will not buy it from you unless it's already working – in other words they will not buy the idea but they might buy the business.

Once you have protection and a prototype or evidence you need to start looking at companies that you want to sell to. Chances are you will already have a company in mind. The more companies you target the more chance you have of being successful. Before you even start contacting them you need to research them all thoroughly. You need to know such things as:

- **Company structure** – who's the best person to talk to? Who makes the decision ultimately? You will have to talk to more than one person and it may well be that you are given a slight run-around at first until you capture one persons interest. Note; if you get too much of a run around then it may well be that you are better off taking your idea somewhere else.

- **Company size** – while large companies have a lot of advantages such as good manufacturing and distribution operations they also usually have the large R&D departments mentioned earlier on. Smaller companies will have less money to invest in R&D and may be more willing to talk to you. It may also be a lot easier to identify the person you need to talk to when dealing with a smaller company.

- **Company Reputation** – find out what sort of reputation the company has. Is it noted for being ethical, does it treat its partners and the people that work for it well? It really is worth knowing as much about the company you are dealing with.

- **Current company products** – this is one that a lot of people seem to forget even though its common sense. The more your product fits in with a company's current product range the more likely it is that they will be interested.

Once you have identified the companies you're interested in and done your research on them you need to prepare your approach. The first thing is to develop a presentation. This will incorporate a lot of the information that you gathered in the Idea Checker stage. You will certainly want to include:

- The issue/problem/need that your idea answers/solves – stressing any USPs (Unique Selling Point – those features that differentiate your idea from your competition and make it stand out).
- Market information including its size, geography and how your idea compares to the competition.
- The manufacturing process – is it complex or simple, are special materials or components required? What costs are involved?
- Protection – how is your idea protected?

A fact sheet along with a working model would look extremely professional.

Once you have your presentation you then contact the companies you are targeting. There are any number of ways to do this. It may well be over the phone or through an email. It may be that there is trade association or convention that you can attend. Some companies hold events for the purpose of meeting with people like you to give them the chance to show off their wares. If you have to send an email or use the phone then give very few details of the actual idea. State simply that you have an idea that does X, is legally protected and that you would be interested in meeting to discuss the possibilities.

If they arrange a meeting, you need to realise a number of things:

- Although you may be attached to your idea and all the details thereof, they will not be interested in those technical details at first. What they will want to know is what it can do for them. How will it help them corner a particular market? How will it help them beat their competition? How will it get them more customers? What you have to realise is that once you get to this point in the process you need to become a salesman. This is where all your research becomes useful.
- There are likely to be a number of meetings and each time you may well be selling your idea to a different person. You need to be patient. The chances are that you will have to travel through

- a series of these meetings to convince them that you really have something, before you finally meet the main decision maker.
- Once negotiations begin in earnest, you would be advised to seek legal advice. There are no set rules when it comes to this stage.

Case Study

Sam, 22, is a magician who specialises in close-up magic. He makes money by performing at a wide variety of events and also by selling his tricks. He says that it's harder to come up with new tricks than it is to sell them because you have to be completely original. Sam is a prolific inventor of new tricks and has his own techniques for ideas generating, which in the grand tradition of magicians everywhere he will not divulge to anyone!

Sam: You have to "re-invent the wheel" to really stand out. I didn't start out to sell my ideas or tricks (because it's the actual trick you sell – not the idea of it, which has to exist first). The first one I sold was a trick called *Paperclip* which I made up when I was sixteen. I'm not too proud of it now to be honest. I created a video of me performing the trick and then stuck it on YouTube. Within six months there'd been seven thousand viewings. A production company got in touch with me by email and said that they would like to buy the trick. I was a bit shocked when they offered me a lump sum payment for the rights to it so I took them up on the offer. I produced a PDF document detailing the effect and they turned it into a booklet and sold it. My main regret over this is that I sold it to a company I had no knowledge of. All I knew was that they were based in Europe. The product that they produced with my name on the front of it was not the quality I wanted.

Four months after *Paperclip* was released I went to university and found myself struggling financially. I came up with a new trick called *CiVIL* (Coin in Very Interesting Location), which is basically a coin-to-shoe trick. As I was desperate for cash I went to the same production company as previously and agreed the same deal with them. The quality of the product was, once again, disappointing but as soon as you sell the rights you have no say in it. The one thing I did differently, however, was to get professional legal advice before I signed on the dotted line. The first time I looked to my parents for advice. Obviously they were not legal experts and took the view that if the company have offered money then I should do it. The second time, I talked to a law professor who looked over the contract for me. I learnt from these two deals to take my time and not sell any of my ideas to the first people that came along.

The next time I sold an idea I planned to sell it. It was called *Card Change* and it involves money falling off of playing cards and business cards. I partnered-up with another young magician, told him about my idea and he helped me develop it further – he basically helped me take it from an idea to an effect. We filmed the trick in action with an aim to selling it. We realised that it was commercial as it utilised a magicians business card, which means that when the magician performs the trick he is also marketing himself to a potential new customer.

I sent the film of me performing the trick to all the production companies that we knew of, which were high quality, big players in the magic world – I wasn't willing to compromise on quality again! This time I also met with many of the people who owned or worked for these companies so was able to gauge how well they would work with us.

Within twenty-four hours we had replies from three of the companies. They were all interested in buying the trick and working with us. Over time we whittled it down to one. They said that the trick was great but that it needed a few tweaks for it to fulfil its commercial potential. We met with them and between us we threw a few ideas around to improve the trick. We then sent them the improved effect and hey presto!

If I had to give advice to anyone it would be to do your homework! Learn as much as you can about the company you've approached or that approached you. Don't be star-struck – as I was at first – because someone has taken an interest in you.

Also it pays to know the face of the person you are dealing with. When I sold my first two tricks I communicated with the buyer through email and I don't think you can make any judgement on emails.

I would definitely recommend that you get legal advice – if you use your brain then it's amazing how much you can get for free.

The last thing I would say is to be as professional as you can! For the last effect that I sold I had a professional film-maker film me doing the trick on an actual stage and then had it professionally edited. I want everything attached to my name to be as professional as possible.

FOURTEEN

HOW TO ENCOURAGE YOUR EMPLOYEES TO BE CREATIVE

I BELIEVE THAT CREATIVE THINKING in a business context should do the following:

- Save money
- Make money
- Save time
- Increase efficiency

In my opinion nowhere will these be better realised than in your workforce. Teaching your employees to think more creatively will give your business a number of benefits which I listed in the introduction to this book. Let's go over them again:

- **They create more products and services** – creative thinkers are always coming up with new ideas – as we will see not all of them are good! In fact some of them will be terrible but the more ideas they come up with the more chance there will be that they will hit on something worth looking at more closely and possibly patenting.

- **They keep on improving their existing products and services** – the creative mind is always looking to improve things – to make things more efficient, you have come across techniques in this book that will make you look critically at what you are currently doing. Creative thinkers are highly analytical and have a questioning attitude.

- **They make more money** – by extending product ranges and improving services a creative workforce can make a business more money.

- **They gain more respect in their industry** – they are able to attract better partners and employees – to have a creative workforce you need to take a small risk and let them have some freedom in the workplace. This space to be creative and the fact that your company will bring out more innovations and constantly improve old products will make you stand out and attract partners and employees in equal measure.

Before we start, however, we need to talk about something that is fundamental to a business and needs to exist before you can develop creativity in your workforce. Quite simply the people you have working for you need to buy into what you are doing and your plans for the business. If they are merely there for the pay and have no real feelings regarding the business then the chances are they will never become creative employees – at least not in the way you want them to be! To develop a creative workforce or work-team you need to ensure that you have the following in place:

- An environment conducive to creativity.
- A system that teaches your work team to be creative.
- A system to recognise and reward creativity.

Environment

This actually has more to do with an approach rather than any actual physical changes to the current work environment. There are a number of steps that you need to take. First of all though let's look at the enemies of creativity in the workplace.

Blocks to creativity

- **Fear of questioning/need to conform** – many people do not deal well with questioning those who they perceive as authority figures. Many do not want to stand out or are scared of rebuke.

- **Fear of lack of structure** – creative thinking encourages ambiguity and the pulling down or questioning of old structures. A lot of people need structures in place and are uncomfortable without them. Many people also dislike ambiguity, (which is an excellent breeding ground for creativity).

- **Fear of failure or looking stupid** – This can be common, particularly if someone is asked for ideas in an area they know little about (as has already been noted, you do not need to be an expert in the area you trying to think creatively about – in fact a little naiveté can be a good thing).

- **Involuntary/forced participation** – I am all for motivating people and making them strive to achieve greater things for themselves and the organisation they work for but if they do not want to take part then you cannot force them. Creative thinking has to be a voluntary activity.

- **Cynicism by authority figures** – if senior managers sneer at the concept of creative thinking many employees will be deterred from participating in it.

Some suggestions to counter the above include:

- Make your employees aware of the fact that you want them to be creative – that you want them to come up with ideas. Send round an email, put up posters and make announcements.

- You need to give them reasons why – tell them the benefits that indulging in creative thinking will bring, on both a personal and professional level.

- You need to show them how this drive for creative thinking fits into your business/company strategy and prove to them that it's not just a management fad.

- A lot of companies offer small amounts of money for those employees that come up with good ideas but very few offer those employees the resources and controls to take their idea forward and see where they get with it. Very few companies offer their employees the chance to interact with other departments and people to bring an idea to life. Imagine the experience that that employee would gain and how much more valuable they would be to you afterwards. In terms of personal and staff development this has to be the ultimate. Obviously you won't do this for every idea that crosses your desk – the idea will need to be reviewed and judged but for those that sound promising let the creator take ownership.

- If you have a mission statement or set of company values, creativity should be mentioned in them.

- Those who want to take part need to be equipped with the basic creative thinking techniques demonstrated in this book and on the website.

- You need to encourage each person to master their current role and study it. Get them to ask awkward questions about it – how they could change things for the better.

- Establish an ideas judgement panel – this should be composed of various people who will change depending on the idea. These people will have the knowledge to know whether or not the idea is viable.

- Encourage your staff on a daily basis and make a big thing of it when one of them comes up with an idea. Express the fact to them quite strongly that you're not just paying lip service to creative thinking – you really want them to act on it.

- A big one is that you need to take away their risk! Make sure that they realise that there is very little risk on their part – if an idea does not work then that is fine – the important thing is that they try.

- Start encouraging your staff to use the question "why?" intelligently – get them to apply it to each other's roles as well as their own.

- Encourage competition between people, teams and departments. Have prizes at various levels for those people who come up with the best ideas and who make them work. Have competitions for those teams or employees who fulfil their ideas quotas. The mind is a goal/direction finding machine, so by giving yourself and your staff a goal you concentrate the mind and help with creativity.

- Make them realise what creativity really is and the personal benefits for them. You will need to bolster their belief in their own creativity.

- Provide your employees with opportunities for creative thinking – come to them with problems that your company is facing and encourage discussion. Even if you already have (or think you have) answers give them a chance to think about it.

- Have regular creative thinking lessons during lunchtime where you teach them techniques and put them into action.

- Display all the intelligent ideas in an area where everyone can see them – be this on the office wall or the company intranet. Everyone should be able to see the latest creative thoughts of their peers.

A System

To be effective a system for creativity needs to:

- Be simple enough to be understood by everyone – go through the system with your team/workforce and map it out for them. Ensure that they all understand it.

- Provide measurable and visible results – if ideas are being fed into the system but none of them are implemented then people will quickly lose morale and creativity will be killed.

- Provide feedback – time should be given over to providing the originator of the idea with honest feedback.

- Be effectively promoted – everyone in your workforce should know about the system.

- Be supported by senior management – senior management should be seen to voice their support for the system.

- Have ideas implemented quickly – slowness in implementing ideas once they have been accepted will have a similar effect on creativity as when there are no visible results at all.

With the above in mind here are my thoughts on creating a system for encouraging the growth of a creative workforce.

When most people think about a system for creativity in the workplace they usually think of the ideas box. I can't think of anything less likely to inspire creativity that the dreaded ideas box. I dislike it because to my mind it creates a barrier. In all likelihood not many people will use it and those who do will most likely suspect that no-one ever reads the ideas. It's very similar to those large wooden thermometers that they stick outside churches when raising money for a new roof. Two years later the red line hasn't gone up any!

- **Communication encourages creativity** – Rather than have them put their ideas into a box give them access to you – let them book an appointment with you to discuss their ideas, which is also a good way of identifying those individuals who are naturally creative.

- **Mix and Match** – Get into the habit of mixing people up in terms of jobs. I once worked in a timber shop buying in timber for the carpenters to make furniture and kitchenware with. I happened to be in a meeting where the team were discussing a problem. One of their clients wanted more space in the cupboards and based on their original design the team couldn't work out what to do. I instantly saw a way in which they could give the client what he wanted. I knew nothing about making cupboards and that's why I was able to make new connections. As long as your staff remember to be non-judgemental of ideas initially this is a very powerful way of encouraging creativity. This is very similar to a technique that I call Expert/Naive.

- **Expert/Naive** – Take someone who has an in-depth knowledge of their role and their part in the structure. They also need to be able to describe exactly what it is they do so that a layman can understand them. Pair them up with someone who knows nothing of that role and get the expert to explain it to them. Because it will be new to the layman his or her brain, provided the role is adequately described to them and they have an interest in it, will simplify any processes involved and often use a metaphor to describe it by comparing it to something they are familiar with. It is here that the potential for creative thinking lies. Such comparisons between what are, on the face of it, unconnected things, can lead to innovation.

- **Focus Groups** – Everyone seems to groan at the thought of focus groups but they are fantastic for ideas generation. People tend to feed off each other, shaping and modifying ideas as they are verbalised. The trick to keeping focus groups is just that – the attendees need to be kept focused and be well managed.

- **Staff Role Swaps** – This is not always possible but encouraging staff to try out each other's roles for a day or two allows them all to gain a new perspective of the business.

- **Company visits** – if you have the resources and the industry/sector in which you work permits it, then it would be worth allowing your employees to visit other companies and see what they do and how they do it. For example I wonder what someone from the car industry could learn from the aerospace industry. I imagine there could be some very fertile land for creativity in such a thing.

- **Away Days** – While the away day has become something of a cliché and is often seen as something of a jolly they can be extremely valuable. A day away from the distractions of the office in a new environment can be extremely beneficial. If planned properly everyone should have them in their diaries so that they have the time to do some research and preparation on the issues that will be being discussed.

The Creative Manager

By now you will have realised that your role as manager/boss is to facilitate the creativity of your team/staff members. A creative manager/boss will:

- Realise when he or she is undermining/blocking the team's creativity and take steps to stop it. There will be times when you want to criticise or judge the ideas your team are coming up with – bite your lip and let them carry on – see what happens.

- Encourage his or her team to constantly ask the question "why?". Get your staff to question why they do things the way they do them – that includes their daily routine from when they enter the workplace to when they leave it.

- Encourage the team to come up with more than one solution to any one problem. By asking for multiple solutions you are getting them to apply a bit more thought to things and encouraging them to make new connections.

- Report the benefits of creative thinking to senior managers – As soon as good results are seen it is important that you let your bosses know how they happened.

- Get to know each of his or her team members one-to-one and facilitate their particular brands of creative thinking. Everyone is creative whether they realise it or not. Your job as their manager is to find out how to switch their creativity on.

- Encourage ownership of ideas. Once a member of staff comes up with a good idea encourage them to develop it further. If it needs the assistance of other departments then encourage them to contact them.

- Award intelligent creative thinking – it's important, even if there are no good results, that your staff are rewarded for having been willing to participate in a creative thinking session.

- Creates an environment conducive to creativity.

- Will challenge his staff with open questions and stress the need for open mindedness.

- Will measure his or her own creative thinking and seek to improve it.

- Strive to embed creativity into the working culture.

- Encourage open communication.

You have probably noticed that all of the above are characteristics of a good manager/boss. Raising your staff's creativity levels will cost you little and the potential returns can be massive. In the current economic climate I honestly believe that no company can afford to block or neglect creative thinking.

FIFTEEN

PERSONAL CREATIVITY FOR BUSINESS

A good manager/boss:

- Is effective at building and maintaining relationships with staff and colleagues.
- Has the ability to see other people's points of view.
- Has a good level of self knowledge.
- Has the ability to motivate staff.
- Empowers his staff thus allowing them to develop themselves.

The techniques we look at in this chapter will help you to become a more effective manager. Remember that these are only examples – it is up to you to find applications for the techniques.

Idea Mapping with Employees for personal development

If you have already tried out the exercises you will know that Ideas Mapping is very powerful – its gets results fast. For certain employees – particularly those who have little direction or motivation – it can be fantastic when you are planning their personal development and career with them. The principles are exactly the same as if you were attempting to come up with a business idea.

When you are using it for yourself or with an employee you need to focus on the following areas:

- Values
- Passions
- Hobbies
- Strengths
- Weaknesses
- Anger/Frustration
- Necessity

All the rules apply but what you will do is ask them more personal questions centred around them as an individual rather than a market or customer. Chances are they will hesitate more when trying to answer your questions but keep up the pressure and keep things going fast to ensure that they focus. By the end of a session you should have the following information:

- Their ambitions.
- Their needs in terms of their job.
- What they believe their strengths and weaknesses are.
- What frustrates them and makes them angry in their every day work life.
- What they think they could do to change things and make them happier.

As a manager/boss would it not be extremely valuable to know all of the above? Having done this you can then help your employee to move forward in a way that makes them happy and ensures their value to the organisation.

Case Study

Lisa works in local government and has a number of people under her. One of them, a young man who had been one of her star members of staff underwent a dramatic change.

Lisa: This young man was one of the most motivated people I had ever worked with. He had a huge amount of energy and was very goal orientated. In six months he had achieved more than some who had been in the organisation for twice that period. He was also really good with people – he got on well with everyone in the team and was excellent at making relationships with people. In short, this young man was capable of going places. Then one day he just changed. He came into the office with a face like thunder, started acting up during meetings and began to be late for work. At first I let it pass because he was so good at what he did and everyone has periods where they find things difficult but this became a constant thing. Within a fortnight my star member of staff had turned into my nightmare. I asked him what the problem was but he honestly couldn't seem to articulate an answer and really didn't seem to know why he was behaving like this. So I decided to use Ideas Mapping in an effort to get to the bottom of it. One of the things that I like about Ideas Mapping is that for some reason it teases things out of people, dredges things up from their unconscious mind. I decided that I had two goals for this Ideas Mapping session:

- One: to tease out from him what the problem actually was.
- Two: to work out how to deal with it and get my star employee back again.

I explained to him what we were going to do and all the rules. He was a little reluctant as it can seem an odd thing to do but he agreed to do it. We did a forty-five minute session. In that session we ran through everything from his passions to his hobbies to the things that frustrated him and made him angry. As we went on mapping these things out we both realised that he was sick of achieving some great things and not getting what he considered to be the right level of attention. For example a project in which he had made a huge contribution reached the regional papers but he didn't feature in any of them. Also another member of staff – a quiet woman who was very competent at her job had been promoted for a job that he felt he should have got based on the results he had been getting. We also realised that he could not admit these feelings to either himself or me because he considered them to be low and dishonourable – not adult. We had a heart to heart and I explained why certain things had happened and we worked out a way for him have a higher profile within the team. We also decided that he needed to work on a few things if he wanted to be promoted.

The one big thing for me was how critical it was for me to ask the right questions. I really had to listen to the answers he was giving me and think about the question. At the end we were both exhausted but happy that we now had a way forward. I honestly believe that if we had not had the Ideas Mapping session I would have lost a very valuable member of staff.

Ideas Mapping with yourself for personal development

Of course you can also do this to yourself. Earlier on in the book I advised you to have a partner for this exercise and I still do – but you can, at a pinch, do this one yourself. You will be amazed at the insights you come up with.

A personal example: A few years ago I did a job I loved, for an organisation of which I was proud to be a member, in a place that I thought was amazing. In my own mind I was living the dream. High on my values column is making an impact and I had a need to do something different every day; this job was fulfilling those criteria for me. Better yet, I was promoted and started to climb the ladder. One day I woke up to find myself depressed and de-motivated. I no longer enjoyed the job. I hated paper-work and, as a manager there was plenty of it! I hated having to organise other people, which my job involved plenty of and I hated sitting in the office all day, which seemed to be my natural place as manager. I missed working on the frontline with the clients. I had taken myself out of my dream job and gone into one that I hated. If I had done this exercise I would have seen within minutes that my ambition (to be a manager) was not confluent with my values, necessities, strengths and weaknesses. I wasn't wrong to be ambitious – I just focused on the wrong way to channel it. Using Ideas Mapping I realised the reason I felt so bad.

By the way if you have children who are planning their careers or what university course to take – or even whether to go to university at all – then this is a great exercise to do with them.

The Five-Sided Technique

The problem with problems is that to some extent they reinforce themselves. Or rather the way we view them reinforces them. Too often without even realising it we solidify a problem or challenge in our minds and then focus on it and try to solve it. If we could view it from a different angle then we are likely to solve it a lot quicker. The five-sided technique is good for solving any type of problem and for making improvements to a product or service. Simply put take your problem and write it in five different ways – I often use this shape to do it. The more ways you have of viewing a problem the more solutions and innovations you can come up with. This can be effective when working with your workforce and they are facing a challenge. For example, say you have been asked to look at ways to save money. You could do the following:

- How can we save money?

- How can we increase the long term financial efficiency of the department?

- How can we spend less money and not damage department efficiency?

- How did other departments in the company save money?

- How did departments in other companies save money and not affect their efficiency or staff morale?

The ways in which you can change the initial view of the problem you have include the following:

- Turn it into a statement and an action: Example "We need to save money by turning off all the lights and cutting down on paper usage."

- Introduce new words: "How can we save money and ensure we do things even better?"
- Replace original words with new ones "How can we be more careful with our money?"

By changing the question you change your perspective and gain new thoughts. Another way of doing this is through perceptual positioning.

Perceptual Positioning

This is an NLP technique that if used correctly is very powerful. It's a technique that my good friend Rintu Basu uses when showing people his model of persuasion. In this book we are going to apply it to business ideas, product improvement and communication. It's really very simple – you can do it in your mind, on paper or use actual people.

In this diagram we have three positions:

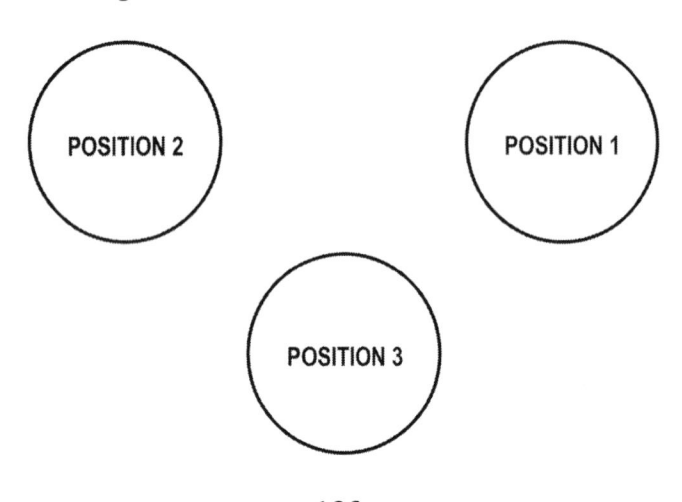

POSITION 2   POSITION 1

POSITION 3

In NLP, Position 1 would be you and your view on a particular problem or issue. Position 2 would be the other person involved in that problem or issue and their views on it. Position 3 is the outside observer looking in and watching the situation. He is neutral and had no particular view at this time. Position 1 (you) will state your view on things and the reason why. Once you have done this you will move to Position 2 and take on the persona of the other person. You will put their viewpoint across and strive to understand the reasons and arguments upon which they base their opinion. You then move into Position 3 and become the disinterested observer and see what insights and what things strike you as being significant.

You could use this technique to look at improving products with Position 1 being you, position 2 being the customer and position 3 being a detached inventor. Imagine using this technique to understand your customer better or your competitor or your boss. Would this help you in your communications with your boss and customers? You may not like your boss any more than you did beforehand but you will understand him better.

Case Study

Judy wasn't happy at work.

Judy: The first six months had been pretty good. I got on with everyone and I did a good job. Pretty soon, though, I began to realise that one of my colleagues, a woman who I'd rather not name, seemed to have to be in control of everything. She was obviously a control freak, albeit a very subtle one. I got on with my manager, which this woman resented slightly – especially as I was doing a really good job and was getting a lot of attention from my colleagues. She began to have meetings with my boss and pretty soon was asking to be more involved with my project. She did it in a really nice way and there were times when I thought I was being paranoid but it soon became obvious that she was trying to gain control over everything. I didn't say anything to my boss but began to feel really bad-tempered. This woman was moving in on my territory and what's worse my boss didn't even seem to realise it and was letting it happen. It started to affect my work as she started to do things that I should be doing and my boss thought she was fantastic. After a few months of this I couldn't even meet this woman's eyes and I was starting to feel bad about my boss who just couldn't see what was going on. I decided to use perceptual positioning to see if I could gain insights into the situation that I could use to my advantage.

First of all I started off in Position 1 as me. I was bad tempered because I was doing really good work and someone else was trying to join in. The insights I gained from this was that I wasn't the best team player and in actual fat was a bit of a loner. If I was being honest with myself (and you have to be for this technique to work) then I was feeling threatened by this woman and was reacting towards her in a fairly hostile manner which wasn't helping the situation. I also realised that I needed to be a little bit more confident about the quality of work and just more confident in myself. To some extent my reactions regarding this situation came about because I had a lack of confidence.

I then moved over to Position 2 and became the woman. I had been working at that place for a while and had been top dog. I had a need to be in control because I wasn't that confident and was scared of being left out. A new person, a new woman to be exact, had come in and started doing really good work. Not only that but she was fairly aggressive, seemed really confident and was capturing everyone's attention. I'm not very creative and she's got lots of good ideas. She's already started a new type of activity – one that I would like to get involved with because I have been doing the same thing for over twelve months and like variety. I work really hard and feel that I should be noticed more, so this may be a way of getting that attention.

Having done this I then moved to Position 3 – the outside observer. I witnessed two people who appeared more confident that they actually are, both of whom want to be noticed. These two are reacting to each other because of their insecurities. Yes there is some power play and manipulation going on but this too is because of their insecurity. The two of them working together could probably achieve a hell of a lot. There is also a bit of a lack of responsibility on the part of Position 1. She needs to stop sulking and start being a little bit more assertive, which is different from aggression.

By using this technique I feel I gained real insights into my own personality and that of the woman. Because of this I began to see a different side to her and could see some vulnerability instead of some confident superwoman. I also realised that although I was doing a good job I could communicate better with my boss. For example he was big on bullet point plans so I started doing more of these and updating him every few days on what I was doing. I decided to stop sulking and take control. I went to my boss and suggested to him that the woman and I could work together on a new activity I had planned. I had worked it all out for him – he thought it was a great idea and it gave her a new area to look at but I made sure that I remained in control of it. Things are now a hell of a lot better than they used to be – not perfect but a lot better and I feel that I have gained in confidence.

The Perfect X

This is exactly the same as the Perfect Day exercise that you will find in a lot of self-help books and is completely opposite to the Negative Thinking technique. It can be applied to just about anything but in this book we will apply it to services and products. It may seem slightly childish but it's actually amazingly powerful. It's very simple and can be done anywhere at any time. All you have to do is daydream about the perfect product for X or the perfect service. As you think about it more intensely, you begin to notice certain features of the product. For this technique to work you have to completely let go of your critical faculties and not worry about whether or not something is possible. The aim is not to achieve the impossible but to come up with those small amendments (in some they may be major) that would really improve things.

Male into Female and vice versa

What would happen if most male mechanics took a little time out to try and imagine themselves as female customers? I'd certainly be interested to see the result. Attempting to see things from the point of view of the other gender can lead to all sorts of ideas for improving services and products. Before you can do this though, you need to get into role.

Imagine yourself as a member of the opposite sex. Picture yourself in the following scenarios:

- Walking into a room full of the opposite sex none of whom you know.
- Meeting up with a group of friends of mixed gender.
- Meeting up with a group of friends, all of whom are of that same gender you are imagining.
- Meeting up with a group of friends, all of whom are of the opposite gender to that which you are imagining.
- Going on a date with a member of the opposite sex.
- Using your product/service as a member of the opposite sex.
- Managing team members of mixed gender.

The insights you will gain from imagining these scenarios and the thoughts and feelings that you will 'remember' can then be carried over into a business context, be that product/service improvement, innovation or relationships.

SIXTEEN

FINAL WORDS

IN THIS BOOK YOU HAVE access to techniques that can help you not only generate viable business ideas but will also help you be a better boss or manager. As I said in the introduction, these techniques can be used for far more than business and, if used intelligently, are useful for improving all areas of life.

So often when people hear the phrase "creative thinking" they identify it with something intangible or "airy fairy" that results in little more than wild "blue sky" ideas. Having read this book you will realise that creative thinking is actually a vital part of business (and life).

I would encourage you to find as many applications for these techniques as you can and show them to other people. There are many resources you can use to find out more about creative thinking and how it can benefit your life and business including my website www.ideasmapping.com. For other resources and books check out the bibliography at the back of this book.

Finally if you have found the information and techniques in this book useful and got the results you wanted I would love to hear about it. I can be reached at josephbenn@ideasmapping.com

BRILLIANT BUSINESS IDEAS

RESOURCES

THERE ARE HUNDREDS OF THOUSANDS of books on the many facets of business. Here are the ones that I personally like.

Business Plans

The Best Laid Business Plans: How To Write Them How To Pitch Them by Paul Barrow

The Business Plan Workbook: The Definite Guide to Researching, Writing Up and Presenting a Winning Plan by Colin Barrow, Paul Barrow, Robert Brown and IoD

Setting Up Your Business

How To Start Your Own Business for Entrepreneurs by Robert Ashton

The Entrepreneurs Book of Checklists by Robert Ashton

Spare Room Start Up: How to Start a Business from Home by Emma Jones

Start Your Own Business in 2011: How to Plan, Fund and Set up a Successful Business by Startups.co.uk

Working 5 to 9: How to Start a Successful Business in Your Spare Time by Emma Jones

The *"Financial Times" Guide to Business Start Up 2010: The Only Annually Updated Guide for Entrepreneurs* by Sara Williams

Selling and Negotiation

Persuasion Skills Black Book: Practical NLP Language Patterns For Getting The Response You Want by Rintu Basu

Bare Knuckle Negotiation: Knockout Negotiation Tactics They Won't Teach You At Business School by Simon Hazeldine

Bare Knuckle Selling: Knock out Sales Tactics They Won't Teach You At Business School by Simon Hazeldine

Lifestyle and business

Screw Work Lets Play: How To Do What You Love And Get Paid For It by John Williams

The 4-Hour Work Week: Escape the 9-5, Live Anywhere and Join the New Rich by Timothy Ferriss

Websites

There are as many websites as there are books on business. Here are those that I use regularly.

For general business support, advice and networking:
http://www.britishchambers.org.uk
http://www.fsb.org.uk

http://enterprisenation.com
http://www.businesslink.gov.uk/bdotg/action/home
http://www.startups.co.uk

For financial and tax queries:
http://www.hmrc.gov.uk/index.htm

For people wanting to change their lifestyles and set up a business:
http://www.fourhourworkweek.com
http://www.screwworkletsplay.com

For business ideas being made a reality around the world, check out:
http://www.springwise.com

ABOUT THE AUTHOR

Joseph Benn is an enterprise support professional currently working and living in the North West of the UK. He has previously worked in the corporate world and academia. He considers himself to be a highly creative thinker who also takes massive amounts of action. This is his first book and it's based around a workshop he designed and has delivered to hundreds of people. Interested in ideas, and new ways of thinking that affect the bottom line in both life and business he writes a blog www.ideasmapping.com.

FREE BRILLIANT BUSINESS E-COURSE

This course builds upon the techniques in the book focusing in on some key areas in more depth. We will also be exploring ways to help you make your ideas a reality quickly and easily.

www.ideasmapping.com/brilliant-business-e-course

Password: i2d3e4a5

Printed in Great Britain
by Amazon.co.uk, Ltd.,
Marston Gate.